VEGETABLES
Canadian Living's™ best

BY
Elizabeth Baird
AND
The Food Writers of Canadian Living Magazine
and The Canadian Living Test Kitchen

A MADISON PRESS BOOK
PRODUCED FOR
BALLANTINE BOOKS AND CANADIAN LIVING™

Ballantine Books
A Division of
Random House of
Canada Limited
1265 Aerowood Drive
Mississauga, Ontario
Canada
L4W 1B9

Canadian Living
Telemedia
Communications Inc.
25 Sheppard Avenue West
Suite 100
North York, Ontario
Canada
M2N 6S7

Canadian Cataloguing in Publication Data

Vegetables

(Canadian Living's best)
Includes index.
ISBN 0-345-39804-1

1. Cookery (vegetables). I. Title.
II. Series.

TX801.B35 1995   641.6'5   C95-930521-1

EDITORIAL DIRECTOR: Hugh Brewster
PROJECT EDITOR: Wanda Nowakowska
EDITORIAL ASSISTANCE: Beverley Renahan
PRODUCTION DIRECTOR: Susan Barrable
PRODUCTION COORDINATOR: Donna Chong
BOOK DESIGN AND LAYOUT: Gordon Sibley Design Inc.
COLOR SEPARATION: Colour Technologies
PRINTING AND BINDING: Friesen Printers

CANADIAN LIVING ADVISORY BOARD: Elizabeth Baird, Bonnie Baker Cowan, Anna Hobbs,
Caren King, Greg MacNeil

CANADIAN LIVING'S™ BEST VEGETABLES
was produced by Madison Press Books
under the direction of Albert E. Cummings

Madison Press Books
40 Madison Avenue
Toronto, Ontario, Canada
M5R 2S1

Printed in Canada

Contents

Introduction 5

Main Dishes 6

Sensational Side Dishes 24

Soups and Starters 50

Seasonal Salads 70

Preserves and Sauces 80

Credits 90

Index 92

Introduction

Ask "What's for supper?" in today's households and chances are you'll hear dishes that include vegetables in a starring role.

That's because, more and more, we're learning to love our vegetables — and catching on to just how important they are to our good health and enjoyment of life. Vegetables figure prominently in Canada's new Food Guide to Healthy Eating, and Canadians are urged to consume between 5 and 11 servings of vegetables and fruits every day!

Now, if vegetables meant only boiled and buttered peas and carrots 5 to 11 times a day, every day of the year, no amount of fiber content or promise of improved night vision could lure us to the produce counter. Thankfully, Canada is blessed with an amazing range of vegetables that are available to us, both at the height of their season and year-round. With so many different flavors, textures and colors to choose from, it's easy to be creative with vegetables in quick-to-make soups, inventive salads and appetizers, tangy sauces and preserves — and, best of all, in a main course.

The blending of cuisines in Canada from around the world has also introduced us to many new vegetables and to well-seasoned ways of serving them up. I hope the recipes you find in *Canadian Living's Best Vegetables* will tempt you to enjoy more vegetables, more often. So when you hear, "Asparagus for supper," it's off with the coat and straight to the table!

Elizabeth Baird

Bowl-of-Jewels Borscht
(recipe, p. 59)

Main Dishes

Now's the time to stir more vegetables into a casserole, toss some into a frittata or make them the highlight of a pasta or pizza — then see what a delicious difference it makes when roots, tubers, seeds, leaves and stalks take center stage at mealtime.

Sweet Peppers with Rice and Sausage ▶

Robust is a good word to describe this colorful and fine-tasting stuffed pepper dish. All you need to add to the menu is a romaine lettuce and cucumber salad with a drizzle of ranch dressing and maybe a sprinkle or two of chives.

2	sweet red peppers	2
2	sweet green or yellow peppers	2
	STUFFING	
2 tbsp	butter	25 mL
1 cup	finely chopped onions	250 mL
2	large cloves garlic, minced	2
12 oz	Italian sausages (sweet or hot)	375 g
1-1/4 cups	parboiled rice	300 mL
1 cup	diced seeded peeled tomatoes	250 mL
2-1/2 cups	beef stock	625 mL
1/3 cup	finely chopped fresh parsley	75 mL
1 tsp	chopped fresh marjoram (or 1/2 tsp/2 mL crumbled dried)	5 mL
Pinch	pepper	Pinch
1/4 cup	freshly grated Parmesan cheese	50 mL
	Salt	
2 cups	shredded mozzarella cheese	500 mL

● STUFFING: In large heavy saucepan, melt butter over medium heat; cook onions and garlic, stirring occasionally, for about 4 minutes or until softened.

● Discard casings from sausages. Add meat to pan, breaking up with back of spoon; cook for 6 to 8 minutes or until meat is no longer pink. Stir in rice until coated; cook for 1 minute.

● Add tomatoes, 2 cups (500 mL) of the stock, parsley, marjoram and pepper; cover and bring to boil. Reduce heat to low, simmer for about 20 minutes or until rice is tender and liquid has been absorbed. With fork, stir in Parmesan. Season with salt to taste.

● Meanwhile, cut peppers in half lengthwise; remove seeds and membranes. In large pot of boiling water, cook peppers, covered, for 5 minutes. Drain and place, cut side down, on racks; let drain.

● Arrange peppers, cut side up, in single layer in large shallow greased baking dish. Fill with rice mixture. *(Recipe can be prepared to this point, covered and refrigerated for up to 3 hours.)*

● Pour remaining stock around peppers. Cover with foil. Bake in 350°F (180°C) oven for 30 minutes. Sprinkle with mozzarella; bake, uncovered, for 5 minutes or until cheese has melted. Broil for 2 to 3 minutes or until cheese is golden brown. Makes 4 servings.

Easy Garden Risotto ▲

Risotto is a rice dish with its roots in the rice-growing region of the Po Valley in Italy. It is usually stir-cooked with stock and wine and a selection of the following — mushrooms, seafood, cheese and vegetables — until flowing and velvety. This easy-fix version requires virtually no stirring.

2 tbsp	olive oil	25 mL
1	large onion, chopped	1
2	cloves garlic, minced	2
1 lb	baby carrots, trimmed	500 g
2 cups	Arborio rice or Italian short grain rice	500 mL
8 cups	(approx) chicken or vegetable stock, heated	2 L
1 lb	asparagus	500 g
1 cup	fresh shelled peas	250 mL
1 cup	chopped green onions	250 mL
1/2 cup	shredded fresh basil	125 mL
1/2 cup	freshly grated Parmesan cheese	125 mL
1 tbsp	lemon juice	15 mL
	Salt and pepper	

● In large heavy saucepan, heat oil over medium heat; cook onion, garlic and carrots, stirring occasionally, for about 10 minutes or until onion is tender.

● Stir in rice and half of the stock; bring to boil, stirring often. Reduce heat to low; simmer for 15 minutes.

● Meanwhile, trim asparagus; cut into 1-inch (2.5 cm) lengths. Add to pan along with half of the remaining stock. Simmer for 10 minutes.

● Stir in peas and remaining stock; simmer for 10 minutes or until vegetables are tender, mixture is creamy and rice is still slightly firm to the bite.

● Stir in green onions, basil, Parmesan, lemon juice, and salt and pepper to taste. Serve immediately. Makes 4 servings.

Garlicky Broccoli Pasta

5 cups	penne (about 1 lb/500 g)	1.25 L
3 cups	broccoli florets	750 mL
3 tbsp	butter	50 mL
3	cloves garlic, minced	3
	Pepper	

● In large pot of boiling salted water, cook penne for 5 minutes. Add broccoli; cook for 3 minutes or until pasta is tender but firm and broccoli is tender-crisp. Drain well.

● Meanwhile, in small saucepan, heat butter with garlic for 2 to 3 minutes or until garlic is softened. Toss with pasta mixture. Season with pepper to taste. Makes 4 servings.

Here's a quick trick that saves on time and dish washing — cook pasta and a vegetable together, in the same pot. For extra oomph, toss with 1/2 cup (125 mL) freshly grated Parmesan.

Tomato Red Pepper Pasta

2 tbsp	olive oil	25 mL
1	onion, chopped	1
1	clove garlic, minced	1
2	sweet red peppers, chopped	2
5	plum tomatoes, chopped	5
1/2 cup	chopped fresh basil	125 mL
1	bay leaf	1
3/4 tsp	salt	4 mL
Pinch	hot pepper flakes	Pinch
	Granulated sugar	
1 lb	spaghetti or linguine	500 g

● In Dutch oven, heat oil over medium heat; cook onion, garlic and red peppers, stirring often, for 10 minutes.

● Add tomatoes, basil, bay leaf, salt and hot pepper flakes; cover and cook over medium-low heat, stirring often, for about 20 minutes or until tomatoes are softened. Discard bay leaf. Purée in food processor or blender. Add sugar to taste.

● Meanwhile, in large pot of boiling salted water, cook spaghetti for 8 to 10 minutes or until tender but firm; drain well and toss with sauce. Makes 4 servings.

Red pepper adds depth and richness to a tomato sauce that's excellent on pasta with a shower of Parmesan. It also layers beautifully in lasagna or tops pizza, fish, or chicken with pizzazz.

Microwave Spaghetti Squash with Cheese

1	spaghetti squash (about 3-1/2 lb/1.75 kg)	1
1/4 cup	butter	50 mL
1/2 cup	cream cheese, cubed	125 mL
2 tbsp	grated Romano cheese	25 mL
2 tbsp	light cream	25 mL
	Salt and pepper	
1/4 cup	each chopped green onion and toasted walnuts	50 mL

● Pierce squash in 4 places. Microwave at High for 4 minutes; turn over and microwave for 4 minutes. Let stand for 10 minutes.

● Cut squash in half lengthwise; remove seeds. Cover with vented plastic wrap; microwave each half at High for about 4 minutes or until fork can ease out strands. With fork, pull out strands and return to shells; cover and keep warm.

● In 8-cup (2 L) microwaveable casserole, microwave butter at High for 25 seconds. Add cream cheese; microwave at High, stirring three times, for about 1-1/2 minutes or until softened. Whisk in Romano cheese and cream.

● Stir in squash until coated. Season with salt and pepper to taste. Serve sprinkled with onion and walnuts. Makes 4 servings.

Spaghetti squash is a novel and fresh alternative to pasta. To jazz up the cheese sauce, grate in a little extra Romano or some Parmesan.

Vegetarian Cabbage Rolls

In the fall, when cabbage is king, roll the leaves around a rice and vegetable stuffing and bake under a soothing blanket of tomato sauce. Since the oven is on, why not bake a panful of apples or pears, too?

1	head cabbage	1
3 tbsp	butter	50 mL
1 tbsp	vegetable oil	15 mL
1	leek, thinly sliced	1
2	cloves garlic, minced	2
1 cup	finely diced carrots	250 mL
1 cup	finely diced peeled rutabaga	250 mL
2-1/2 cups	cooked short grain rice	625 mL
1/4 cup	each chopped fresh parsley and dill	50 mL
1/2 tsp	dried marjoram	2 mL
1/2 tsp	salt	2 mL
1/4 tsp	pepper	1 mL
1	can (14 oz/398 mL) tomato sauce	1
1 tbsp	packed brown sugar	15 mL
1 tbsp	cider vinegar	15 mL

● Trim and core cabbage. In large pot, cover cabbage with boiling water; let stand for 8 to 10 minutes or until outer leaves can easily be removed. Carefully remove 12 leaves; dip each leaf into boiling water for 3 minutes or until softened.

● In large skillet, melt 2 tbsp (25 mL) of the butter with oil over medium heat; cook leek and garlic, stirring occasionally, for 3 minutes or until softened.

● Add carrots and rutabaga; cover and cook over medium-low heat for 3 minutes. Remove from heat; stir in rice, parsley, dill, marjoram, salt and pepper.

● Spoon mixture onto cabbage leaves, using about 1/2 cup (125 mL) for large leaves and 1/3 cup (75 mL) for small ones. Roll up leaves, tucking in sides; arrange in greased 13- x 9-inch (3.5 L) baking dish.

● Brush rolls with remaining butter. Combine tomato sauce, sugar and vinegar; spoon over rolls. Cover and bake in 350°F (180°C) oven for 1-1/2 hours. Makes 6 servings.

Cabbage Roll Casserole

Just imagine coming home on a bone-chilling day to find the kitchen warm and inviting with the aroma of cabbage rolls. That's the magic — and convenience! — of a Crockpot. This hearty meal is packed with all the flavor of traditional cabbage rolls, but it's a lot easier to make.

1-1/2 lb	hot Italian sausages	750 g
2	large potatoes	2
2	onions, chopped	2
4	cloves garlic, chopped	4
4	carrots, sliced	4
1	can (10 oz/284 mL) chicken stock	1
1	can (19 oz/540 mL) tomatoes, chopped	1
2 tbsp	chopped fresh dill (or 1 tbsp/15 mL dried dillweed)	25 mL
1/2 tsp	each caraway seeds, celery seeds and salt	2 mL
1/4 tsp	each pepper and nutmeg	1 mL
4 cups	coarsely sliced trimmed cabbage	1 L
1/2 cup	coarsely chopped fresh parsley	125 mL
2 tbsp	butter	25 mL

● Discard casings from sausages; cut into bite-size chunks. In skillet, brown sausages over medium-high heat; drain off fat and transfer sausages to Crockpot.

● Meanwhile, peel potatoes; grate 1 and dice 1. Add to Crockpot along with onions, garlic, carrots, chicken stock, tomatoes, dill, caraway and celery seeds, salt, pepper and nutmeg. Cover and cook over low heat for 7-1/2 hours.

● Add cabbage, parsley and butter, pushing cabbage down into liquid; cook for 30 to 60 minutes or until vegetables are tender. Makes 6 servings.

TIP: This recipe was developed for a large (4.5 L) Crockpot; halve the recipe if your Crockpot is 3.5 L or less.

Cauliflower and Broccoli Medley

1	head each cauliflower and broccoli, cut into florets	1
1 cup	cubed cooked ham (8 oz/250 g)	250 mL
Pinch	paprika	Pinch
	CHEESE SAUCE	
2 tbsp	butter	25 mL
3 tbsp	all-purpose flour	50 mL
1-1/2 cups	milk	375 mL
1 cup	shredded Cheddar cheese	250 mL
Dash	hot pepper sauce	Dash
1/4 tsp	each salt and pepper	1 mL

● In pot of boiling water, cook cauliflower for 4 to 6 minutes or until tender-crisp; remove with slotted spoon and drain. Add broccoli and cook for 2 to 3 minutes or until tender-crisp; drain.

● CHEESE SAUCE: Meanwhile, in saucepan, melt butter over medium heat; blend in flour and cook, stirring, for 2 minutes. Gradually whisk in milk; cook, whisking, for 3 to 4 minutes or until thickened. Remove from heat; stir in Cheddar until melted. Add hot pepper sauce, salt and pepper.

● Pour one-third of the sauce into 11- x 7-inch (2 L) greased baking dish. Layer cauliflower, then half of the ham over sauce; pour another third of the sauce over top. Add broccoli and remaining ham; spoon remaining sauce over top. Sprinkle with paprika. *(Dish can be prepared to this point, covered and refrigerated for up to 8 hours; add 10 minutes to baking time.)*

● Bake in 350°F (180°C) oven for about 30 minutes or until heated through. Makes 4 servings.

Cheese sauce and cubed ham (leftover is ideal) transform two cabbage-family favorites into a tempting one-dish supper. For a vegetarian version, simply omit the ham.

CLOSE-UP ON CAULIFLOWER

Choose Well
● The best cauliflowers have compact white heads and crisp green leaves clinging to the stem end.

● Avoid cauliflower with yellowed heads and a strong smell.

Quantity
● A medium cauliflower weighs a generous 1-1/2 lb (750 g) and serves four.

Storage
● Wrap in toweling, enclose in plastic bag and refrigerate whole for up to 1 week. Use cut pieces within 2 days.

Preparation
● Trim leaves off stalk and trim away stalk and core. Divide curd (the white florets) into bite-size pieces, trimming off white stalks.

Cooking Basics
● Cook florets, covered, in 1 inch (2.5 cm) boiling water for 4 to 6 minutes or until tender-crisp. Or, steam for about 10 minutes.

● A whole head can be boiled or steamed, in about double the time it takes to cook florets.

Nutrition Note
● An excellent source of vitamin C and folate.

● Cauliflower is a cruciferous vegetable which may help to protect against certain cancers.

Mellow Onion and Provolone Pizza

Here's a pizza with style and class — the kind you can't order in — and one that's worth the time to make at home. Skip the homemade base if you're pressed, and use bought pizza dough or a prebaked base. If the base is prebaked, take 5 minutes off the baking time.

1 tsp	granulated sugar	5 mL
1 tsp	active dry yeast	5 mL
1 cup	(approx) all-purpose flour	250 mL
2 tbsp	(approx) cornmeal	25 mL
1 tbsp	olive oil	15 mL
1/2 tsp	salt	2 mL
	TOPPING	
4 tsp	olive oil	20 mL
6 cups	sliced onions (about 5 large)	1.5 L
4	cloves garlic, slivered	4
1	bay leaf	1
1/2 tsp	dried oregano	2 mL
1/4 tsp	each salt and pepper	1 mL
1-1/2 cups	shredded sharp provolone cheese	375 mL
1/3 cup	slivered black olives	75 mL

● In food processor, combine 1/2 cup (125 mL) warm water, sugar and yeast; let stand for 10 minutes. With motor running, add flour, cornmeal, oil and salt, processing just until dough forms ball.

● Turn out dough onto lightly floured surface; knead into smooth ball. Place in lightly greased bowl, turning to grease all over. Cover and let rise for 30 minutes.

● TOPPING: Meanwhile, in large skillet, heat oil over medium heat; cook onions, garlic, bay leaf, oregano, salt and pepper, stirring often, for 20 minutes or until onions are golden and tender. Let cool slightly; discard bay leaf.

● Sprinkle 12-inch (30 cm) round pizza pan with cornmeal. On floured surface, roll out dough and fit into prepared pan. Spread with one-third of the provolone cheese, the onion mixture, olives, then remaining cheese.

● Bake on lowest rack in 500°F (260°C) oven for about 15 minutes or until crust is golden and cheese has melted. Makes 4 servings.

Sliced Potato Pizza ▶

Potatoes star in both the pizza crust and the topping. Rosemary's the herb of choice, and the layers of potato slices are graced with assertive provolone and Parmesan cheeses.

5	potatoes	5
1	onion, thinly sliced	1
2 tbsp	olive oil	25 mL
Half	sweet red pepper, slivered	Half
2	cloves garlic, minced	2
1 tbsp	minced fresh parsley	15 mL
1/2 tsp	salt	2 mL
1/4 tsp	each dried rosemary and pepper	1 mL
1/2 cup	shredded provolone or mozzarella cheese	125 mL
1/4 cup	freshly grated Parmesan cheese	50 mL

● Scrub potatoes and slice thinly. In bowl, toss together potatoes, onion and oil. Stir in red pepper, garlic, parsley, salt, rosemary and pepper.

● Brush 12-inch (30 cm) round pizza pan with oil; spread with potato mixture. Bake in 450°F (230°C) oven for 15 minutes or until tender, brown and crisp.

● Sprinkle with provolone and Parmesan cheeses; bake for 5 to 8 minutes or until golden brown. Makes 6 servings.

Potato and Mushroom Strudel

Scaramouche Restaurant in Toronto serves an excellent potato strudel which we've adapted here. It can be a dazzling main dish or a side dish for a special-occasion dinner.

1 tbsp	butter	15 mL
1	onion, sliced	1
1	clove garlic, minced	1
1 cup	sliced mushrooms	250 mL
2-1/3 cups	diced potatoes (about 4)	575 mL
1 tbsp	chopped fresh thyme	15 mL
2 tbsp	water	25 mL
1/4 cup	freshly grated Parmesan cheese	50 mL
1	green onion, chopped	1
	Salt and pepper	
4	sheets phyllo pastry	4
1/4 cup	butter, melted	50 mL

● In large skillet, melt butter over medium heat; cook onion, garlic and mushrooms, stirring often, for 5 minutes or until liquid has evaporated.

● Stir in potatoes and 2 tsp (10 mL) of the thyme. Add water; cover and cook for 8 to 10 minutes or until potatoes are tender. Remove from heat. Stir in Parmesan, green onion, and salt and pepper to taste. Let cool.

● Place one sheet of phyllo on work surface, keeping remaining phyllo covered with damp tea towel. Brush sheet lightly with butter. Layer remaining phyllo on top, brushing each sheet with butter.

● Spoon potato mixture over phyllo, leaving 2-inch (5 cm) border along one long side and 1-inch (2.5 cm) border at each short end. Starting at other long side, carefully roll up jelly roll-style, folding in edges while rolling. Place, seam side down, on greased baking sheet. Brush with butter.

● Bake in 400°F (200°C) oven for 18 to 20 minutes or until golden-crisp. Let stand for 5 minutes. Sprinkle with remaining thyme. Slice diagonally with serrated knife. Makes 4 servings.

CLOSE-UP ON POTATOES

Choose Well
● Choose firm potatoes without sprouts and blemishes, avoiding ones tinged with green. This indicates the presence of solanine, a naturally occuring toxin produced when potatoes are exposed to light. Check potatoes carefully if they've been packaged in clear plastic.

Quantity
● Three medium potatoes total about 1 lb (500 g) and yield about 3 cups (750 mL) sliced or cubed and 2 cups (500 mL) mashed.

● Count on 1 medium to large potato per serving.

● Ten to 12 new potatoes weigh about 1 lb (500 g) and serve two to three.

Storage
● Never in plastic and not in the refrigerator.

● Choose a cool, dark and well-ventilated spot, away from onions which promote rot in potatoes.

● Thick-skinned mature potatoes keep for up to 2 weeks. For storage up to 3 months, temperature should be around 50°F (10°C).

Preparation
● Scrub potatoes with stiff brush; trim out eyes. Leave peel on new potatoes and on potatoes used for salads (to hold their shape better).

● If peeling, do so just before cooking.

Cooking Basics
● To boil, place in saucepan of cold water, cover and bring to boil. Reduce heat slightly and boil for about 20 minutes or until tender. Drain, returning pot to heat for a few seconds to dry potatoes.

● To bake, prick in several places and bake on rack in 400°F (200°C) oven for about 45 minutes or until potato yields to gentle pressure. Do not bake in foil.

● To microwave, pierce potato and microwave at High for 4 minutes or until potato yields to gentle pressure. Add 2 to 3 minutes for each additional potato.

Nutrition Note
● With skin on, potatoes are a powerhouse of vitamin C and, even without skin, are rich in potassium.

Potato Casserole with Cheese and Mushrooms ▲

2	large baking potatoes	2
3/4 tsp	salt	4 mL
2 tbsp	olive oil	25 mL
2 cups	sliced mushrooms	500 mL
1/2 cup	freshly grated Parmesan cheese	125 mL
1	onion, sliced	1
2	cloves garlic, minced	2
1 tbsp	chopped fresh parsley	15 mL
1/2 tsp	dried thyme	2 mL
1/4 tsp	pepper	1 mL
2 cups	shredded mozzarella cheese	500 mL

● Peel and cut potatoes into thin slices. In bowl, toss potatoes gently with 1/2 tsp (2 mL) of the salt and half of the oil.

● In separate bowl, toss together mushrooms, half of the Parmesan, the onion, garlic, parsley, thyme, pepper and remaining salt.

● In 8-cup (2 L) greased casserole, arrange one-third of the potatoes in slightly overlapping layer; cover with half of the mushroom mixture, then one-third of the mozzarella. Repeat layers. Arrange remaining potatoes over top; sprinkle with remaining mozzarella and Parmesan cheeses. Drizzle with remaining oil.

● Bake in 400°F (200°C) oven for 40 to 45 minutes or until tender. Let stand for 10 minutes. Makes 4 servings.

From the rustic cooking of Tuscany comes this deeply satisfying potato casserole. Add grilled Italian sausages to the menu, if you like — or serve as is with a crisp salad for a vegetarian supper.

Zucchini, Potato and Egg Skillet Supper

At the end of the week, when there are only a few eggs, straggler potatoes and a zucchini or two lurking in the crisper, here's how to put them together quickly in a tasty fuss-free supper.

1/4 cup	butter or olive oil	50 mL
2	potatoes, peeled and diced	2
2-1/2 cups	coarsely grated zucchini	625 mL
1/4 cup	chopped fresh chives or green onions	50 mL
4	eggs	4
	Salt and pepper	

● In 10-inch (25 cm) heavy skillet, melt half of the butter over medium heat; cook potatoes, stirring often, for about 5 minutes or until tender. Add zucchini and chives; cook, stirring, for 1 minute.

● In large bowl, beat eggs lightly; stir in vegetables. Season with salt and pepper to taste.

● Wipe out skillet and melt remaining butter; pour in egg mixture. Reduce heat to medium-low; cook, shaking pan occasionally, for about 5 minutes or until bottom is lightly browned. Cover and cook for 5 to 6 minutes longer or until top is firm. Serve in wedges. Makes 4 servings.

Asparagus Frittata

Fresh asparagus and eggs are splendid spring brunch fare. When fresh isn't available, use frozen and defrost only long enough for ice crystals to disappear.

2 tbsp	butter	25 mL
1	small onion, chopped	1
2 cups	diagonally sliced blanched asparagus	500 mL
2 cups	shredded Swiss cheese	500 mL
1/4 cup	chopped chives or green onions	50 mL
6	eggs	6
1/2 cup	fresh bread crumbs	125 mL
1/2 tsp	salt	2 mL
Dash	hot pepper sauce	Dash
Pinch	Pepper	Pinch

● In 6-cup (1.5 L) microwaveable quiche dish or deep pie plate, cover and microwave butter and onion at High for 2 to 4 minutes or until softened. (Or, cook in skillet over medium heat for about 5 minutes.) Arrange asparagus, Swiss cheese and chives over top; set aside.

● In bowl, beat eggs; stir in bread crumbs, salt, hot pepper sauce and pepper; pour over asparagus mixture. Bake in 350°F (180°C) oven for 25 to 30 minutes or until set in center. Let stand for 10 minutes before serving. Makes 8 servings.

Plum Tomato and Capocollo Flan

1-1/2 cups	fresh bread crumbs	375 mL
1	clove garlic, minced	1
3 tbsp	freshly grated Parmesan cheese	50 mL
2 tbsp	olive oil	25 mL
1 tsp	chopped fresh rosemary (or 1/2 tsp/2 mL dried)	5 mL
1/4 tsp	pepper	1 mL
3 oz	provolone cheese, sliced	75 g
3 oz	mozzarella cheese, sliced	75 g
6 oz	capocollo ham, sliced	175 g
6	firm plum tomatoes	6
1 tbsp	chopped fresh parsley	15 mL

● Spray nonstick coating onto bottom and side of 9-inch (23 cm) tart pan with removable bottom. In bowl, combine bread crumbs, garlic, Parmesan, oil, rosemary and half of the pepper.

● Reserve 2 tbsp (25 mL) of the crumb mixture; press remaining crumb mixture firmly onto bottom and halfway up side of pan. Bake in 400°F (200°C) oven for about 8 minutes or until light golden.

● Stack provolone and mozzarella cheese slices; cut into wedges. Stack capocollo; cut into wedges. Slice tomatoes. Arrange alternating slices of cheese, ham and tomatoes around edge of crust. Repeat with remaining slices to form second ring inside.

● Combine reserved crumb mixture with parsley; sprinkle over flan. Season with remaining pepper. Bake in 400°F (200°C) oven for 5 minutes; reduce heat to 350°F (180°C) and bake for 20 to 25 minutes longer or until heated through and cheese is bubbly. Let cool on rack for 10 minutes. Makes 4 servings.

F*resh bread crumbs are essential to the success of this crispy-bottomed pie. Make them by crumbling slices of bread and whizzing in a food processor or blender until fine.*

SUN-DRIED TOMATOES

● Sun-dried tomatoes deliver an extra wallop of flavor to pasta sauces, stews, pizza toppings and salad dressings. Whether packed in oil or loose in bags, dried tomatoes have gone from an exotic ingredient in specialty stores to one that's widely available in the produce section of major supermarkets.

● To rehydrate the dry-packed variety, let stand in very hot water for 20 minutes.

● To make your own dried tomatoes, core and cut plum tomatoes into quarters; place, cut side up, on baking sheets. Bake in 200°F (100°C) oven for about 6 hours or until withered.

Tomato and Basil Tart ◄

1 cup	ricotta cheese	250 mL
3/4 cup	grated Asiago cheese	175 mL
1/4 cup	chopped fresh basil	50 mL
2	egg yolks	2
1/2 tsp	salt	2 mL
Dash	hot pepper sauce	Dash
4	plum tomatoes, thinly sliced	4
1 tbsp	olive oil	15 mL
	PASTRY	
1-2/3 cups	all-purpose flour	400 mL
1/2 tsp	dried thyme	2 mL
1/4 tsp	salt	1 mL
2/3 cup	shortening	150 mL
1	egg yolk	1
1 tsp	white vinegar	5 mL
	Ice water	

● PASTRY: In bowl, stir together flour, thyme and salt; with pastry blender or two knives, cut in shortening until crumbly. In measuring cup, blend together egg yolk, vinegar and enough ice water to make 1/2 cup (125 mL); sprinkle over flour mixture, tossing with fork until dough holds together. Press into disc; wrap and chill for 30 minutes.

● On lightly floured surface or using pastry cloth and stockinette-covered rolling pin, roll out pastry to 14-inch (35 cm) circle; fit onto 12-inch (30 cm) round pizza pan.

● In bowl, stir together ricotta cheese, 1/4 cup (50 mL) of the Asiago cheese, basil, egg yolks, salt and hot pepper sauce; spread over pastry.

● Arrange tomatoes over top, pressing gently. Brush tomatoes with oil; sprinkle remaining Asiago cheese around border. Fold pastry border over filling. Bake in 425°F (220°C) oven for 25 minutes or until crust is golden. Makes 6 servings.

TIP: Other cheeses such as Gruyère, Cheddar or fontina can replace the Asiago.

Fresh from the oven, this fragrant and cheesy tomato-topped pie just begs to be cut and enjoyed right away. Garnish with a few sprigs of fresh basil and serve a leaf lettuce salad with lemon vinaigrette alongside.

Cheddar-Corn Impossible Pie

2 tbsp	dry bread crumbs	25 mL
10	slices bacon, cooked and crumbled	10
1 cup	shredded mild Cheddar cheese	250 mL
1	onion, finely chopped	1
Half	sweet green pepper, diced	Half
1 cup	corn kernels	250 mL
Pinch	salt	Pinch
1/4 tsp	pepper	1 mL
Pinch	cayenne pepper	Pinch
1/2 cup	all-purpose flour	125 mL
1 tsp	baking powder	5 mL
2 tbsp	shortening	25 mL
4	eggs	4
2 cups	milk	500 mL

● Grease 10-inch (25 cm) quiche pan or pie plate; sprinkle with bread crumbs. Combine bacon, Cheddar, onion, green pepper, corn, salt, pepper and cayenne; sprinkle over bread crumbs.

● In bowl, stir together flour and baking powder; cut in shortening until in fine crumbs. Add eggs and milk; whisk just until smooth. Pour over bacon mixture.

● Bake in 350°F (180°C) oven for 45 to 50 minutes or until knife inserted near center comes out clean. Let stand for 5 minutes. Makes 4 servings.

The flour mixture in this vegetable-packed supper dish magically forms a very thin tender base for its zesty custard filling. Serve with salsa or chili sauce and a broccoli and carrot slaw.

Cornmeal Corn Pancakes

These pancakes are a guaranteed kid-pleaser, and make a quick supper with sliced tomatoes and ham.

TIP: If using frozen corn, thaw quickly in the microwave or in a sieve in cold water. Drain well.

1/2 cup	all-purpose flour	125 mL
1/2 cup	cornmeal	125 mL
1 tbsp	granulated sugar	15 mL
1 tsp	baking powder	5 mL
1/2 tsp	baking soda	2 mL
1/4 tsp	salt	1 mL
1	egg	1
1 cup	plain yogurt	250 mL
1/4 cup	milk	50 mL
4 tsp	vegetable oil	20 mL
1/2 cup	corn kernels	125 mL

● In bowl, stir together flour, cornmeal, sugar, baking powder, baking soda and salt. Whisk together egg, yogurt, milk and half of the oil; pour over flour mixture. Add corn and stir just until blended.

● Brush large nonstick skillet with some of the remaining oil; heat over medium-high heat. Using 1/4 cup (50 mL) batter for each pancake, cook for 2 to 3 minutes or until golden brown on bottom; turn and cook for 1 minute longer. Makes 4 servings.

Corn Custard Pudding

Vegetables, especially corn, baked in a savory custard make the kind of light supper dish that appeals to children. Or, you can serve this as a side dish with pork chops, ham steaks or chicken.

3	eggs	3
1-1/2 cups	corn kernels	375 mL
1 cup	milk or light cream	250 mL
1 cup	shredded Swiss cheese	250 mL
1/2 cup	chopped green onions	125 mL
1/4 cup	chopped sweet red pepper	50 mL
1/4 cup	all-purpose flour	50 mL
1 tsp	salt	5 mL
1/4 tsp	pepper	1 mL
Pinch	dried thyme	Pinch
1/2 cup	cracker crumbs or dry bread crumbs	125 mL
2 tbsp	butter, melted	25 mL

● In large bowl, whisk eggs; stir in corn, milk, Swiss cheese, onions and red pepper. Whisk in flour, salt, pepper and thyme. Pour into greased 6-cup (1.5 L) soufflé dish or casserole. Toss crumbs with butter; sprinkle over corn mixture.

● Place dish in larger pan; pour in enough boiling water to come halfway up side of dish. Bake in 375°F (190°C) oven for 50 to 60 minutes or until puffed and knife inserted in center comes out clean. Makes 4 to 6 servings.

CLOSE-UP ON LEEKS

Choose Well
● Leeks with the longest white in proportion to the coarser green stalk are the most desirable.

● Choose straight firm stalks, with little bulging at the root end, and crisp green leaves showing no signs of wilting or browning.

Quantity
● One bunch (usually 3 leeks) weighs about 1-1/2 lb (750 g) and produces about 3 cups (750 mL) chopped white leek.

Storage
● Wrap in toweling, enclose in plastic bag and refrigerate for up to 1 week.

Preparation
Trim off limp outer leaves, leaving the root end intact. Trim off flat dark green leaves where they start to pale.

● Slit each leek stalk from green leaf end almost to root end. Holding leek root end up and spreading leaves, flush out grit under cold water.

Cooking Basics
● Leeks are most often used as a flavoring in soups, stews and casseroles. Onions are a reasonable substitute.

Nutrition Note
● Provide some vitamins and minerals to the diet.

Leek Tart ▲

	Pastry for 11-inch (28 cm) tart or quiche shell	
2 tbsp	butter	25 mL
4 cups	chopped leeks (about 5)	1 L
2 tbsp	Dijon mustard	25 mL
5	slices bacon, cooked and crumbled	5
2	eggs	2
1/2 cup	whipping cream	125 mL
1/2 cup	light cream	125 mL
1/4 tsp	pepper	1 mL
Pinch	salt	Pinch

● On lightly floured surface, roll out pastry and fit into 11-inch (28 cm) tart or quiche pan; refrigerate for 20 minutes. Prick bottom with fork; line with foil and fill with pie weights. Bake in 375°F (190°C) oven for 10 minutes. Remove pie weights and foil; bake for 15 minutes longer or until lightly golden. Let cool.

● Meanwhile, in large skillet, melt butter over medium-low heat; cook leeks, stirring occasionally, for about 30 minutes or until softened. Let cool.

● Brush cooled pastry shell with mustard; spread leeks over top. Sprinkle with bacon. Whisk together eggs, whipping cream, light cream, pepper and salt; pour over bacon. Bake in 350°F (180°C) oven for 30 to 35 minutes or until golden. Makes 6 servings.

Well worth making for a special lunch, this rich and savory shallow French pie celebrates the sweetness of leeks. (To make your own pastry, see recipe, p. 19.)

TIP: Use pie weights (available in kitchen shops) or dried beans to prevent crust from shrinking as it bakes. Let weights or beans cool; store and re-use.

Eggplant Rolls with Quick Tomato Sauce

Thin slices of eggplant are wrapped around a creamy mixture of ricotta and provolone cheeses and baked under a blanket of smooth tomato sauce. Serve this vegetarian entrée with crusty Italian bread and a lettuce and mushroom salad.

2	eggplants (about 1-1/4 lb/625 g each)	2
2 tsp	salt	10 mL
1/3 cup	olive oil	75 mL
	Quick Tomato Sauce (recipe follows)	
1/3 cup	freshly grated Parmesan cheese	75 mL
	FILLING	
2	eggs	2
3 cups	ricotta cheese (about 1 lb/500 g)	750 mL
2 cups	shredded provolone or Asiago cheese	500 mL
1/4 cup	finely chopped fresh parsley	50 mL
1/4 cup	thinly sliced green onions	50 mL
1/4 tsp	salt	1 mL
Pinch	each nutmeg, pepper and cayenne pepper	Pinch

● Cut eggplants lengthwise into 1/4-inch (5 mm) thick slices. Layer in colander, sprinkling each layer with some of the salt; let stand for 30 minutes. Rinse well under cold water; pat dry.

● FILLING: Meanwhile, in large bowl, beat eggs; blend in ricotta and provolone cheeses, parsley, onions, salt, nutmeg, pepper and cayenne. Set aside.

● Brush eggplant slices on both sides with oil. Broil on two baking sheets for 2 to 4 minutes on each side or until golden and softened. Let cool.

● Spoon filling evenly onto wide ends of eggplant slices; roll up jelly roll-style. Arrange rolls, seam side down, in 13- x 9-inch (3.5 L) baking dish. Spoon Quick Tomato Sauce over top; sprinkle with Parmesan.

● Bake in 400°F (200°C) oven for 30 to 40 minutes or until sauce is bubbly. Let stand for 5 minutes. Makes 6 to 8 servings.

QUICK TOMATO SAUCE		
1 tbsp	olive oil	15 mL
1 cup	chopped onions	250 mL
2	cloves garlic, minced	2
1	can (28 oz/796 mL) tomatoes	1
1	bay leaf	1
Pinch	each pepper, granulated sugar and dried basil	Pinch

● In saucepan, heat oil over medium heat; cook onions and garlic, stirring occasionally, for 3 minutes or until softened.

● Add tomatoes, bay leaf, pepper, sugar and basil; bring to boil. Reduce heat to low; simmer for 30 minutes or until slightly thickened. Discard bay leaf. Pass through food mill, or purée and press through sieve. Makes about 2-1/4 cups (550 mL).

Curried Winter Vegetables

1 tbsp	vegetable oil	15 mL
1	clove garlic, minced	1
1	onion, chopped	1
4 tsp	curry powder	20 mL
1/2 tsp	salt	2 mL
3	potatoes, peeled and cubed	3
2	large carrots, cubed	2
2 cups	cubed peeled squash	500 mL
2 cups	cauliflower florets	500 mL
1	can (10 oz/284 mL) tomato juice	1
1/2 cup	water	125 mL
1 tbsp	lemon juice	15 mL
1	apple, chopped	1
2 cups	frozen peas	500 mL

● In large saucepan, heat oil over medium heat; cook garlic and onion, stirring often, for 6 to 8 minutes or until golden. Stir in curry powder and salt; add potatoes, carrots, squash and cauliflower, tossing to coat.

● Pour in tomato juice, water and lemon juice; cover and bring to boil. Reduce heat to low; simmer for 15 to 20 minutes or until vegetables are tender.

● Add apple; cover and cook for 5 minutes. Add peas; cook for 3 to 5 minutes or until heated through. Makes 4 servings.

Surround the flavorful curry and rice with small bowls of condiments such as chutney, chopped nuts or fruit, raisins, yogurt and grated carrots.

CLOSE-UP ON WINTER SQUASH

Choose Well
● Select hard-skinned squash without blemishes that feel heavy for their size.

Quantity
● Winter squash vary enormously in size; count on about 1/2 lb (250 g) squash per serving.

● Smaller squash such as acorn are delicious halved and baked to make two generous servings.

● A 2-lb (1 kg) butternut squash yields about 6 cups (1.5 L) cubed and 2-1/2 cups (625 mL) mashed.

Storage
● Store squash for up to several months in a cool, dark and dry spot.

Preparation
● Wash squash; remove stems. Cut squash in half or in chunks depending on size; with sharp spoon, scoop out seeds and fibers.

Cooking Basics
● Bake, cut side down, in greased baking dish in 400°F (200°C) oven for about 45 minutes or until soft.

● Or, steam for about 10 minutes or until tender.

Nutrition Note
● Very high in beta carotene. Provide vitamin C, folate, potassium and fiber.

Keep in Mind
● When a recipe calls for peeled squash, choose smooth-skinned butternut or delicata. Acorn, pepper or sweet dumpling squash are ideal for stuffing.

● For simple baking in halves or chunks, buttercup, banana, hubbard, turban, kuri and other very hard-skinned squash are suitable.

Sensational Side Dishes

If the truth be told, vegetable side dishes should really be called vegetable center dishes, since they now play such an important role in our diets — and add flavor, color, texture and pleasure to any meal.

Sweet and Sour Pearls ▶

Although it takes time to peel pearl onions, they're a delight to eat, especially when braised in this Mediterranean mix of sweet dark or golden raisins and tangy vinegar. Serve hot as a side dish, or at room temperature as an appetizer with cheese or pâté.

8 cups	pearl onions (2-1/2 lb/1.25 kg)	2 L
3	strips orange rind	3
1	bay leaf	1
1 cup	raisins	250 mL
2 tbsp	olive oil	25 mL
2 tbsp	red wine vinegar	25 mL
1 tbsp	tomato paste	15 mL
1/2 tsp	salt	2 mL
1/4 tsp	pepper	1 mL
1	clove garlic, slivered	1

● In heatproof bowl, cover onions with boiling water; let stand for 30 seconds. Drain and peel; cut shallow X in root end of each. In 13- x 9-inch (3 L) baking dish, combine onions, orange rind and bay leaf.

● In saucepan, bring 1 cup (250 mL) water, raisins, oil, vinegar, tomato paste, salt, pepper and garlic to boil; pour over onions.

● Cover and bake in 325°F (160°C) oven, basting and turning in sauce every 30 minutes, for about 2 hours or until onions are tender and sauce has thickened. Discard orange rind and bay leaf. Makes 8 servings.

Balsamic Roasted Onions

Serve these mellow onions with a shave or two of Parmigiano Reggiano and crusty rolls, or pair them with roast chicken, veal or pork.

1/4 cup	olive oil	50 mL
8	large onions	8
1/2 tsp	each salt and pepper	2 mL
2 tbsp	balsamic or red wine vinegar	25 mL
2 tbsp	chopped fresh parsley	25 mL

● In 13- x 9-inch (3 L) baking dish, drizzle oil over onions; sprinkle with salt and pepper. Cover and bake in 375°F (190°C) oven, basting and turning every 20 minutes, for 1 hour.

● Uncover and bake for about 45 minutes or until very soft. Transfer to warmed serving dish. Drizzle with vinegar; sprinkle with parsley. Makes 8 servings.

Herbed Onions and Mushrooms

8	onions	8
2 tbsp	butter	25 mL
1 tsp	granulated sugar	5 mL
1 tbsp	balsamic vinegar	15 mL
3 tbsp	olive oil	50 mL
8 cups	mushrooms (1-1/2 lb/750 g)	2 L
2	cloves garlic, minced	2
1 tsp	dried thyme	5 mL
1/4 cup	chopped fresh parsley	50 mL
	Salt and pepper	

● Quarter onions, leaving root ends intact. In large skillet, melt butter over medium-low heat; cook onions and sugar, stirring occasionally, for 35 to 40 minutes or until tender and golden brown. Transfer to bowl; stir in vinegar. Set aside.

● In skillet, heat oil over medium heat; cook mushrooms, garlic and thyme, stirring occasionally, for about 7 minutes or until moisture has evaporated. Add onions; heat through. Stir in parsley, and salt and pepper to taste. *(Onion mixture can be refrigerated for up to 1 day; reheat gently to serve.)* Makes 8 servings.

Two-Tone Grilled Onion Slices

1	each red and white onion	1
1/3 cup	olive oil	75 mL
1	clove garlic, minced	1
1/2 tsp	dried marjoram or basil	2 mL
1/4 tsp	pepper	1 mL
3 tbsp	balsamic vinegar	50 mL
	Salt	

● Cut onions into 1/2-inch (1 cm) thick slices. Insert toothpick through rings of each slice to hold rings together. Stir together oil, garlic, marjoram and pepper; brush some over onions.

● Place onions on greased grill over low heat; cover and cook, brushing often with oil mixture, for 10 to 15 minutes on each side or until tender. Remove from grill. Brush both sides with vinegar; season with salt to taste. Makes 4 servings.

Sesame Carrots

6	large carrots	6
1 tbsp	sesame seeds	15 mL
2 tbsp	orange juice	25 mL
1 tsp	grated gingerroot	5 mL
1 tsp	sesame oil	5 mL
1 tsp	soy sauce	5 mL
	Salt and pepper	

● Peel carrots and cut into sticks. Cover and steam for about 8 minutes or until tender-crisp. (Or, microwave with 2 tbsp/25 mL water at High for 5 minutes.)

● In small skillet, cook sesame seeds over medium heat, shaking pan occasionally, for 2 minutes or until golden; combine with orange juice, ginger, sesame oil and soy sauce. Toss with carrots; season with salt and pepper to taste. Makes 4 to 6 servings.

Creamed Carrots and Onions

5 cups	pearl onions (1-1/2 lb/625 g)	1.25 L
8 oz	baby carrots	250 g
1/4 cup	butter	50 mL
1/2 cup	finely chopped pecans	125 mL
1/2 cup	bread crumbs	125 mL
2	onions, chopped	2
1/4 cup	all-purpose flour	50 mL
1 cup	milk	250 mL
4 oz	light cream cheese	125 g
	Nutmeg, salt and pepper	

● In heatproof bowl, cover onions with boiling water; let stand for 30 seconds. Drain and peel; cut shallow X in root end of each. Scrub carrots.

● In pot of boiling salted water, cook onions and carrots for 5 to 7 minutes or until tender-crisp; drain, reserving 1 cup (250 mL) liquid. Place vegetables in 6-cup (1.5 L) baking dish.

● In same pan, melt butter; pour half into bowl and toss with pecans and bread crumbs. Set aside.

● In remaining butter in pan, cook chopped onions over low heat, stirring occasionally, for 5 minutes. Sprinkle with flour; cook, stirring, for 1 minute. Increase heat to medium. Gradually whisk in reserved liquid and milk; cook, whisking, for 5 minutes or until smooth and thickened.

● Reduce heat to low; stir in cream cheese until melted. Season with nutmeg, salt and pepper to taste. Pour over onion mixture; sprinkle with crumb mixture. *(Recipe can be prepared to this point, covered and refrigerated for up to 1 day; let stand at room temperature for 30 minutes before baking.)*

● Bake in 350°F (180°C) oven for 20 to 25 minutes or until bubbling. Makes 8 servings.

For holiday entertaining, make-ahead dishes such as this creamy carrot and onion combo are a godsend.

WHICH SIZE TO CHOOSE?
Throughout this book, all vegetables are medium-size unless otherwise specified.

CLOSE-UP ON CARROTS

Choose Well
● In summer, carrots with tops attached are sold bunched. Look for bright orange crisp carrots and perky bright green tops. Straight carrots are easier to peel.

● Carrots sold in plastic bags are usually thicker than bunched carrots with tops, and their shoulders should be dry with no sign of darkening or sprouting.

Quantity
● 1 lb (500 g) carrots will yield about 3-1/2 cups (875 mL) chopped, grated or sliced, and give 3 to 4 servings.

Storage
● Cut or twist tops off to prevent them from draining moisture from the carrots. Wrap loosely in toweling and place in a plastic bag; refrigerate for up to a week.

Preparation
● Scrub fresh-from-the-garden carrots with a stiff vegetable brush under cold running water.

● Peeling is not needed for impeccably fresh or small baby carrots. Peel larger carrots with swivel vegetable peeler and rinse well.

● Cut into coins or sticks for quick cooking, into chunks for roasting or stews. Shred for salads, garnish, pancakes, muffins, cakes and meat loaves.

Cooking Basics
● Cook small whole carrots or slices in a small amount of boiling water, stock, apple or orange juice in covered saucepan until tender-crisp, about 10 minutes for whole carrots, about 8 minutes for slices.

● Watch carrots carefully near end of cooking time to prevent scorching. Or, steam whole in slices, saving any steaming liquid for soups and stews.

Nutrition Note
● Carrots are a rich source of vitamin A, beta carotene and vitamin C. A raw carrot provides 2 g of fiber.

Stir-Fried Sweet and Sour Carrots

10	long slim carrots	10
2	large onions	2
2 tbsp	vegetable oil	25 mL
1	large clove garlic, minced	1
1 tsp	minced gingerroot	5 mL
3/4 cup	chicken stock	175 mL
2 tbsp	packed brown sugar	25 mL
2 tbsp	white or cider vinegar	25 mL
2 tsp	cornstarch	10 mL
3/4 tsp	salt	4 mL
1/4 cup	thinly sliced green onion	50 mL

● Peel carrots and cut diagonally into 1/2-inch (1 cm) thick slices. Slice onions in half lengthwise; slice thinly.

● In wok or large skillet, heat oil over high heat; stir-fry garlic and ginger for 10 seconds. Add carrots and onions; stir-fry for 1 minute. Pour in 1/4 cup (50 mL) of the stock; cover and cook over medium-low heat, stirring occasionally, for 12 to 15 minutes or until carrots are tender.

● Combine remaining stock, sugar, vinegar, cornstarch and salt; pour into wok. Stir-fry over high heat for about 2 minutes or until vegetables are glazed. Serve sprinkled with green onion. Makes 6 servings.

Cutting carrots into even-size chunks is the secret to even cooking.

TIP: For a spicy version, add a few drops of hot pepper sauce or a pinch of cayenne pepper plus 1/2 tsp (2 mL) ground cumin or curry powder to stock.

Curry Glazed Carrots ◄

12	carrots	12
2 tbsp	butter	25 mL
1	clove garlic, minced	1
1 tbsp	chopped gingerroot	15 mL
1-1/2 tsp	curry powder	7 mL
1-1/2 cups	chicken stock	375 mL
2 tbsp	liquid honey	25 mL

● Peel carrots and cut into 1/4-inch (5 mm) thick slices.

● In deep skillet, heat butter, garlic and ginger over medium heat for 1 minute. Add curry powder; cook, stirring, for 30 seconds.

● Add carrots, stock and honey; cook, stirring occasionally, until liquid evaporates and carrots are tender and glazed. Makes 4 to 6 servings.

Curry powder adds just a little mystery to carrots without intimidating either the cook or the diner.

Carrot Pilaf

2 tbsp	butter	25 mL
3	carrots, chopped	3
1 cup	long grain rice	250 mL
1 tsp	ground cumin (optional)	5 mL
2-1/2 cups	chicken stock	625 mL
1/4 cup	chopped fresh parsley	50 mL
	Salt and pepper	

● In large saucepan, melt butter over medium heat; cook carrots, rice, and cumin (if using) for 2 minutes.

● Stir in stock and bring to boil; reduce heat, cover and simmer for about 15 minutes or until rice is tender and liquid is absorbed. Stir in parsley; season with salt and pepper to taste. Makes 4 servings.

Carrots add punch to a pot of rice. For extra flavor, add a chopped onion to the carrots as they sauté with the butter.

Caramelized Beets and Onions (p. 32) and Curry Glazed Carrots

Carrots Moroccan-Style ▲

Carrots are a powerhouse of vitamin A, and one serving packs in all you need for the day. Nutrition aside, carrots are also delicious, especially when they're laced with the Moroccan flavors of cumin, cinnamon and lemon.

3	large carrots	3
1/4 tsp	dried thyme	1 mL
Pinch	each ground cumin, cinnamon and salt	Pinch
2 tbsp	chopped fresh parsley	25 mL
1 tbsp	lemon juice	15 mL
1 tsp	butter	5 mL
1 tbsp	plain yogurt	15 mL
	Pepper	

● Peel carrots and cut into sticks; place in steamer basket. Sprinkle with thyme, cumin, cinnamon and salt. Cover and steam for about 5 minutes or just until tender.

● Transfer to bowl. Mix in parsley, lemon juice and butter; stir in yogurt. Season with pepper to taste. Makes 4 servings.

Roasted Root Vegetables

3	baking potatoes	3
Half	rutabaga	Half
2	carrots	2
1	parsnip	1
1	large onion	1
3 tbsp	(approx) olive oil	50 mL
1	clove garlic, minced	1
1 tsp	dried rosemary	5 mL
1 tsp	coarse salt	5 mL
1/2 tsp	pepper	2 mL

● Peel potatoes, rutabaga, carrots, parsnip and onion; cut into 1-1/2-inch (4 cm) chunks. Combine oil, garlic, rosemary, salt and pepper; toss with vegetables.

● Lightly brush baking sheet with olive oil; place in 425°F (220°C) oven for 3 minutes. Spread vegetables on hot baking sheet in single layer; bake, shaking baking sheet two or three times during cooking to turn vegetables over, for 40 to 45 minutes or until tender and browned. Makes 4 servings.

Imagine a dish of old-fashioned root vegetables that are crispy on the outside and melt-in-your-mouth tender on the inside. That's the magic of high-heat roasting.

Parsnip-Carrot Purée with Apricots

5	parsnips	5
4	carrots	4
2	potatoes	2
1/2 cup	dried apricots	125 mL
3 tbsp	butter	50 mL
1/2 tsp	nutmeg	2 mL
	Salt and pepper	

● Peel and dice parsnips, carrots and potatoes; place in large pot. Add apricots; cover with water and bring to boil. Reduce heat to medium; cook for 25 to 30 minutes or until tender. Drain well.

● In food processor, purée vegetables until smooth; blend in butter, nutmeg, and salt and pepper to taste. Makes 4 servings.

Carrots and their fair-skinned cousins, parsnips, both have a natural sweetness that marries beautifully with tangy apricots.

TIP: Puréed vegetable medleys like this one can be made a few hours ahead and reheated in the microwave or in the top of a double boiler.

Puréed Parsnips with Cumin

6	parsnips	6
1/2 cup	milk	125 mL
3 tbsp	butter	50 mL
1 tsp	ground cumin	5 mL
1/2 tsp	salt	2 mL
1/4 tsp	pepper	1 mL

● Peel and cut parsnips into 1/2-inch (1 cm) cubes. In pot of gently boiling water, cook parsnips for 10 to 12 minutes or until tender; drain well.

● In food processor or with hand masher, purée parsnips with milk, butter, cumin, salt and pepper until smooth. Makes 4 servings.

The earthiness of cumin transforms parsnips into an ever-so-slightly-exotic vegetable guaranteed to jazz up meals for family and friends.

TIP: For a special presentation, use a pastry bag to decoratively pipe parsnip purée onto platter around roasted meat.

Caramelized Beets and Onions

Cooking beets in their skins gives the best color and flavor. You'll know the beets are tender when the skin loosens and is easy to slip off. (Photo, p. 28)

6	large beets	6
4 tsp	butter	20 mL
3	onions, sliced	3
2 tbsp	granulated sugar	25 mL
2 tbsp	red wine vinegar	25 mL
2 tbsp	water	25 mL
1/2 tsp	salt	2 mL
1/4 tsp	pepper	1 mL

● In large pot of boiling water, cook beets for about 40 minutes or until tender. (Or, pierce and microwave with 1/4 cup/50 mL water at High, stirring twice, for 14 to 16 minutes; let stand for 5 minutes.) Drain and let cool slightly; slip off skins and cut beets into sticks.

● Meanwhile, in large nonstick skillet, melt butter over medium heat; cook onions, stirring often, for 7 to 10 minutes or until light golden. Sprinkle with sugar and vinegar; reduce heat to low and cook for about 20 minutes or until tender and golden.

● Add beets to onions along with water, salt and pepper; heat over medium heat for 3 to 5 minutes or until heated through. Makes 4 servings.

Honey-Orange Beets

When fresh beets are not available, canned whole beets are a quick and convenient alternative.

6	beets	6
1 tsp	grated orange rind	5 mL
2 tbsp	orange juice	25 mL
2 tsp	butter	10 mL
1 tsp	liquid honey	5 mL
1/4 tsp	ground ginger	1 mL
	Salt and pepper	

● In pot of boiling water, cook beets for about 40 minutes or until tender. Drain and let cool slightly; slip off skins and cube or slice.

● In saucepan, heat orange rind and juice, butter, honey and ginger over low heat until butter melts. Add beets and toss to coat. Season with salt and pepper to taste. Makes 4 servings.

Beet and Pear Purée

When looking for new ways to enjoy beets, try this vibrant purée mellowed with pears — a perfect dish to complement turkey, chicken or pork.

8	beets	8
1	can (14 oz/398 mL) unsweetened pears	1
1/3 cup	butter	75 mL
1-1/2 cups	chopped onions	375 mL
1/4 cup	red wine vinegar	50 mL
1/2 tsp	salt	2 mL
Pinch	pepper	Pinch

● In large pot of boiling water, cook beets for about 40 minutes or until tender; drain and let cool slightly. Slip off skins; set beets aside.

● Drain and coarsely chop pears, reserving liquid for another use. In large skillet, melt butter over medium heat; cook onions and pears, stirring often, for 10 to 15 minutes or until golden. Add vinegar, salt and pepper; simmer for 30 seconds.

● In food processor or blender, purée beets and pear mixture until smooth. Transfer to 8-cup (2 L) casserole. Cover and bake in 350°F (180°C) oven for 25 to 35 minutes or until heated through. Makes 8 servings.

CLOSE-UP ON PEAS

Choose Well
● Straight from garden to pot is the ideal for peas since their sugar quickly turns into starch.

● Choose crisp bright-green pea pods that are well filled with medium-size peas.

Quantity
● 1 lb (500 g) whole peas yields 1-1/3 cups (325 mL) shelled peas, about 2 servings.

Storage
● Wrap unshelled peas in paper towels, enclose in plastic bag and refrigerate for up to 2 days.

Preparation
● Rinse peas; separate pods to pop peas into waiting bowl.

Cooking Basics
● Cook peas, covered, in 2 inches (5 cm) of boiling water for about 2 minutes. Or, steam for about 8 minutes.

● A touch of sugar in the cooking water blesses the sweetness of all peas.

Nutrition Note
● An excellent source of folate, a good source of fiber and a source of vitamin C and beta carotene.

Gingery Orange Squash Toss

3 cups	cubed peeled squash	750 mL
1/3 cup	orange juice	75 mL
2 tsp	butter	10 mL
1	clove garlic, minced	1
1-1/2 tsp	minced gingerroot	7 mL
	Salt and pepper	

● In large nonstick skillet, combine squash, orange juice, butter, garlic and ginger; cover and cook over medium-low heat, stirring occasionally, for 10 to 15 minutes or until tender. Season with salt and pepper to taste. Makes 4 servings.

For maximum beta carotene, choose squash that's deep yellow or orange inside.

Buttercup Squash and Apple Casserole

2 tbsp	butter	25 mL
1	onion, chopped	1
1	buttercup squash, peeled and cubed	1
1	apple, peeled and sliced	1
1/2 cup	vegetable or chicken stock	125 mL
1/4 cup	apple juice	50 mL
1/2 tsp	ground cumin	2 mL
1/4 tsp	cinnamon	1 mL
	Salt and pepper	
1/2 cup	walnut or pecan halves	125 mL

● In large saucepan, melt butter over medium-low heat; cook onion, covered, for about 8 minutes or until softened.

● Add squash, apple, stock, apple juice, cumin and cinnamon; bring to simmer. Cover and cook over medium heat for about 20 minutes or until squash and apple are tender. Mash until smooth; season with salt and pepper to taste.

● Transfer to greased 8-cup (2 L) baking dish; score top with fork. Arrange walnuts over top. Bake in 400°F (200°C) oven for 20 to 25 minutes or until walnuts are toasted and casserole is piping hot. Makes 8 servings.

Make the most of the fine texture of squash for this oven casserole. Studding the top with walnuts sets this dish up for entertaining.

Honey-Glazed Rutabaga or Turnip

Laced with honey and ginger, both orange rutabaga and white turnips are a delicious foil for chicken, duck and turkey.

2 lb	rutabaga or turnips	1 kg
2 tbsp	butter	25 mL
1/4 cup	liquid honey	50 mL
1/4 tsp	ground ginger	1 mL
	Salt and pepper	

● Peel rutabaga and cut into 1/2-inch (1 cm) thick slices; halve or quarter slices.

In pot of boiling salted water, cook rutabaga for 15 minutes (turnips for 8 minutes) or just until tender; drain.

● Stir in butter; cook over high heat, shaking pan often, for 1 minute or until coated. Stir in honey, ginger, and salt and pepper to taste; cook, stirring often, for 1 minute or until glazed. Makes 4 servings.

Golden Rutabaga Casserole

Rutabaga is all the better when its bitter edge is tempered with other sweeter vegetables such as carrots and toothsome apricots and oranges.

1	orange	1
6	carrots, chopped	6
5 cups	cubed peeled rutabaga	1.25 L
1/2 cup	dried apricots	125 mL
2 tbsp	maple syrup	25 mL
2 tbsp	butter	25 mL
	Salt and pepper	
1/2 cup	sour cream	125 mL
Pinch	each cinnamon and nutmeg	Pinch

● Remove rind from orange; cut into julienne strips. Cut off white pith; chop orange.

● In large saucepan, combine 3 cups (750 mL) water, orange rind, orange, carrots, rutabaga, apricots, maple syrup, butter, and salt and pepper to taste; bring to boil. Reduce heat and simmer for 30 to 40 minutes or until water evaporates and vegetables are tender.

● In food processor, purée mixture in batches, adding sour cream, cinnamon and nutmeg to last batch. Transfer to warmed vegetable bowl and stir. Makes 8 servings.

CLOSE-UP ON RUTABAGA AND TURNIPS

Choose Well
● Most yellow rutabaga are sold waxed. Choose rounded unblemished ones that feel heavy.

● White globe-shaped turnips with their purple crowns should be crisp, firm and smooth-skinned.

Quantity
● Average rutabaga weigh about 1-3/4 lb (800 g) and produce 5-1/2 cups (625 mL) cubed, and 3 cups (750 mL) mashed. Count about 3 servings per lb (500 g).

● Allow one medium turnip per serving.

Storage
● Rutabaga, a dense vegetable, keep well — either in the refrigerator for about 3 weeks, or in a cool, dark, dry and well-ventilated spot for up to 2 months.

● Turnips soften quickly; store in plastic bag in refrigerator for up to 1 week.

Preparation
● Cut slice off bottom of rutabaga; place, cut side down, on cutting board and slice in two. Place each half, cut side down, on board and cut into slices.

● Peel each slice individually; cut slices into sticks or cubes.

● For turnips, simply trim off tops and roots; pare thinly and slice or cube.

Cooking
● Boil or steam cubed rutabaga or turnips or small whole turnips in about 2 inches (5 cm) boiling water for 8 to 10 minutes for cubed turnips, 20 to 30 minutes for whole turnips and rutabaga cubes.

Nutrition Note
● Contribute fiber and are a good source of Vitamin C and potassium.

CLOSE-UP ON EGGPLANT

Choose Well
- Keep a firm, tight, glossy skin in mind when choosing eggplant — whether it's the dark purple globe-shaped variety, the long slim Japanese or any of the other white, green or variegated ones.
- A good eggplant has no rust spots or wrinkles and feels heavy for its size.

Quantity
- Eggplants weigh about 1 to 1-1/2 lb (500 to 750 g). The larger ones yield a generous 6 cups (1.5 L) and serve 4.

Storage
- Wrap in toweling and enclose in plastic bag to store in refrigerator for up to 4 days.

Preparation
- Rinse and remove stem, trimming out blossom end. Peel if indicated in recipe, and slice or cube.
- Layer in colander with light sprinkle of salt and place in sink to drain for about 30 minutes. Rinse quickly and pat dry with towels.

Cooking Basics
- Bake, broil, grill or stew eggplant — avoiding moist methods of cooking.

Nutrition Note
- Not noted for richness in any one vitamin or mineral.

Keep in Mind
- Salting and draining removes moisture from the eggplant and lowers the amount of oil needed to sauté slices.

Turkish Eggplant

3	eggplants (about 1 lb/500 g each)	3
	Salt	
1/4 cup	olive oil	50 mL
6	onions, sliced	6
6	large cloves garlic, minced	6
6	tomatoes, peeled, seeded and chopped	6
1/2 cup	minced fresh parsley	125 mL
2 tbsp	lemon juice	25 mL
	Pepper	
	Freshly grated Parmesan cheese (optional)	

- Cut eggplants in half lengthwise; sprinkle cut sides with salt. Let drain in colander for 45 minutes. Rinse under cold water; pat dry.

- Brush cut sides of eggplants with 1 tsp (5 mL) of the oil. Bake, cut side down, on baking sheet in 350°F (180°C) oven for about 40 minutes or until tender. Scoop out eggplant, leaving 1/2-inch (1 cm) thick shell; set shells aside. Chop eggplant and set aside.

- Meanwhile, in Dutch oven, heat remaining oil over medium heat; cook onions, stirring occasionally, for about 10 minutes or until softened.

- Add garlic and tomatoes; bring to boil. Reduce heat and simmer for 25 to 30 minutes or until thickened. Stir in chopped eggplant, parsley, lemon juice, and salt and pepper to taste.

- Spoon eggplant mixture into eggplant shells; bake on lightly greased baking sheet in 350°F (180°C) oven for 25 minutes or until heated through. Sprinkle with Parmesan (if using). Makes 6 servings.

Our Test Kitchen lightened up this very rich Middle Eastern dish for Canadian Living reader Cecilia Danysk. Instead of the 1 cup (250 mL) oil cooked with a traditional Imman Bayeldi, this new version skinnies the oil down to 1/4 cup (50 mL) without sacrificing any of the flavor.

Garden Vegetable Platter ▶

Vary the flavors and colors of this appealing vegetable dish (featured on the cover), depending on what's in season, and add a summery herb drizzle for an extra burst of flavor.

1	small eggplant	1
1	each green and golden zucchini, thinly sliced	1
8 oz	Italian green beans, trimmed	250 g
8 oz	asparagus, trimmed	250 g
1	each red and yellow tomato, sliced	1
1	sweet green pepper, sliced into rounds (optional)	1
	Fresh basil and oregano	
	Fresh peas	
	DRESSING	
2/3 cup	olive oil	150 mL
1/4 cup	red wine vinegar	50 mL
3 tbsp	chopped fresh oregano	50 mL
2 tbsp	chopped fresh basil	25 mL
1 tbsp	Dijon mustard	15 mL
3	cloves garlic, minced	3
1/2 tsp	each salt and pepper	2 mL

● DRESSING: In small bowl, whisk together oil, vinegar, chopped oregano and basil, mustard, garlic, salt and pepper.

● Cut eggplant into 1/4-inch (5 mm) thick slices. Lightly brush eggplant and zucchini with some of the dressing; place on greased grill over medium-high heat. Grill zucchini for 5 to 6 minutes and eggplant for 10 to 15 minutes, basting with dressing and turning occasionally, or until vegetables are tender.

● Meanwhile, in large pot of boiling salted water, cook beans for 4 to 5 minutes or until tender-crisp. With slotted spoon or tongs, remove to colander; refresh under cold water and drain well.

● Add asparagus to pot. Cook for about 3 minutes or until tender-crisp; drain and refresh under cold water. Drain again.

● Brush tomatoes with 2 tbsp (25 mL) of the dressing; toss beans, asparagus, and green pepper (if using) with remaining dressing. Decoratively arrange over platter along with grilled eggplant and zucchini. Garnish with basil, oregano and peas. Makes 6 servings.

CLOSE-UP ON SUMMER SQUASH

Choose Well
● Summer squash comes in a variety of shapes and colors — from cigar-shaped green and golden zucchini to globe-shaped striped zucchini, yellow straightneck and crookneck squash and scalloped pattypan squash.

● All have a delicate flavor and a similar high moisture content that make recipes for one generally suitable for the others.

● Look for taut-skinned glossy specimens that feel firm and heavy for their size. For all these squash, smaller and younger is always better.

Quantity
● Four small zucchini or pattypan squash total 1 lb (500 g) and provide 3 to 4 servings.

Storage
● Wrap loosely in toweling and enclose in plastic bag; store in refrigerator for up to 3 days.

Preparation
● Under cold water, brush with soft brush; trim off ends.

Cooking Basics
● Boiling or steaming is not recommended because of the high moisture content of all summer squash.

● Instead, grill slices, stir-fry, sauté, bake, include in kabobs or stew with tomatoes, onions, eggplant and garlic.

● Zucchini especially is suited to being grated. Salt and let drain for about 30 minutes in colander. Press out moisture and sauté.

Nutrition Note
● Provides vitamin C, potassium, folate and fiber.

CLOSE-UP ON CABBAGE

Choose Well
- The best green and red cabbages have firm compact heads with shiny leaves.

- Savoy cabbage has a slightly looser head because of its crinkled leaves.

- Long slim napa cabbage has crisp light green and white leaves.

- Choose unblemished heads that feel heavy and have no cabbage odor.

Quantity
- A 1-1/2-lb (750 g) cabbage yields about 8 cups (2 L) shredded, about 6 servings.

Storage
- Refrigerate whole red or green cabbage in plastic bag and use within 1 week.

- Wrap cut portions in plastic and use within 2 days.

- Use whole napa and Savoy cabbages within 4 days.

Preparation
- Remove coarse outer leaves; rinse in cold water. Quarter and cut out core. Shred finely or cut into wedges.

Cooking Basics
- Steam wedges for 10 minutes, or boil in covered saucepan for 5 minutes.

- Shred red cabbage before cooking. To retain color, add a touch of vinegar, wine or apple juice.

Nutrition Note
- Contributes vitamin C and fiber. It is also a brassica vegetable which may protect us from certain cancers.

Red Cabbage with Cranberries

Red on red, this spicy cabbage dish complements pork roasts or chops, ham and poultry — turkey, too! A holiday favorite you'll enjoy serving all through the year.

2 tbsp	butter	25 mL
1 tbsp	vegetable oil	15 mL
1	red onion, chopped	1
14 cups	shredded red cabbage	3.5 L
1/2 cup	cranberry juice	125 mL
1/3 cup	cranberry sauce	75 mL
2 tbsp	red wine vinegar	25 mL
3/4 tsp	salt	4 mL
1/4 tsp	pepper	1 mL
1	bay leaf	1
Pinch	each ground cloves and cinnamon	Pinch

- In Dutch oven, heat butter and oil over medium heat; cook onion, stirring, for 3 minutes or until softened. Add cabbage; cook, stirring, for 2 minutes or until coated.

- Stir in juice, sauce, vinegar, salt, pepper, bay leaf, cloves and cinnamon; bring to boil, stirring often. Reduce heat to low; cover and cook for 45 minutes.

- Uncover and cook for 15 minutes or until cabbage is tender and most of the liquid is absorbed. Discard bay leaf. Makes 8 servings.

Mustardy Brussels Sprouts

This tasty dress-up for brussels sprouts works deliciously on green beans, too.

1-1/2 lb	brussels sprouts, trimmed	750 g
1/4 cup	butter	50 mL
1/4 cup	minced red onion	50 mL
2 tbsp	chopped fresh parsley	25 mL
2 tbsp	Dijon mustard	25 mL
2	cloves garlic, minced	2
1 tbsp	red wine vinegar	15 mL
Pinch	granulated sugar	Pinch
	Salt and pepper	

- In large pot of boiling salted water, cook brussels sprouts for 5 minutes or until tender-crisp; drain.

- In large skillet, melt butter over medium heat; stir in onion, parsley, mustard, garlic, vinegar, sugar, and salt and pepper to taste. Add brussels sprouts and toss to coat well; cover and cook for 2 minutes. Makes 8 servings.

Stir-Fried Cabbage

2 tbsp	vegetable oil	25 mL
1 tsp	black mustard seeds	5 mL
1 tsp	sesame seeds	5 mL
1/2 tsp	cumin seeds	2 mL
1/4 tsp	hot pepper flakes	1 mL
2	onions, halved and sliced	2
6 cups	shredded cabbage	1.5 L
1	sweet red pepper, cubed	1
1/2 tsp	salt	2 mL
2 tbsp	water	25 mL
1 tbsp	lemon juice	15 mL

● In wok or large nonstick skillet, heat oil over medium heat; cook mustard seeds, sesame seeds, cumin seeds and hot pepper flakes, stirring, for 3 minutes or until seeds begin to pop.

● Add onions; cook, stirring, for 4 minutes or until softened. Add cabbage, red pepper and salt; toss to combine. Pour in water; cook, tossing often, for 12 minutes or until cabbage is tender-crisp. Toss with lemon juice. Makes 6 servings.

Overcooking has given cabbage both a bad smell and a bad reputation. Let this quickly cooked cabbage dish with accents of onions and sweet pepper change all that!

Sicilian Broccoli

1	bunch broccoli	1
1/4 cup	fresh bread crumbs	50 mL
2 tbsp	pine nuts	25 mL
2 tbsp	olive oil	25 mL
4	anchovy fillets, minced (or 1/2 tsp/2 mL anchovy paste)	4
1	clove garlic, minced	1
2 tbsp	currants	25 mL
	Salt and pepper	

● Separate broccoli into bite-size florets; peel and slice stems. In large pot of boiling salted water, cook florets and stems for 3 to 4 minutes or until tender-crisp. Drain well and place in bowl.

● Meanwhile, in skillet, toast bread crumbs and pine nuts over medium-low heat, stirring often, for 3 to 5 minutes or until golden. Add to bowl.

● In same skillet, heat oil over medium heat; cook anchovies and garlic for 1 minute. Add to bowl along with currants. Season with salt and pepper to taste; toss well. Makes 4 servings.

Currants and pine nuts, trademarks of Sicilian cooking, add a pleasant sweetness to the dish, while the anchovy, equally Sicilian, balances it off with saltiness and depth.

CLOSE-UP ON BROCCOLI

Choose Well
● Dark green compact florets, clear light green stalks and a clean smell are the signs of fresh broccoli.

● Avoid broccoli with thick woody stems and any sign of yellowing.

Quantity
● One bunch broccoli (2 to 3 stalks) weighs about 1-1/2 lb (750 g), produces about 6 cups (1.5 L) chopped and serves four.

Storage
● Wrap loosely in toweling and place in open plastic bag; refrigerate for up to 3 days.

Preparation
● Trim off bottom of stalk and cut off florets where they spread from stalk. Separate florets into bite-size pieces.

● With vegetable peeler, peel stalk; cut into bite-size pieces. Include leaves, if possible.

Cooking Basics
● Boil, covered, in 1 inch (2.5 cm) boiling water for about 4 minutes or until vivid green and tender-crisp. Or, steam for about 7 minutes.

Nutrition Note
● A powerhouse of nutrients, broccoli is packed with vitamin C, beta carotene, folate, potassium and fiber, and is an important vegetable source of calcium and iron.

Steamed Cauliflower with Thyme Vinaigrette

Present a whole cauliflower in delicious style, drizzled with a herb vinaigrette. Serve warm or at room temperature, basting the head often with the dressing as it accumulates around the base.

1	head cauliflower	1
3 tbsp	white wine vinegar	50 mL
2 tsp	dried thyme	10 mL
2 tsp	Dijon mustard	10 mL
1 tsp	granulated sugar	5 mL
1	clove garlic, minced	1
1/4 tsp	each salt and pepper	1 mL
1/3 cup	extra virgin olive oil	75 mL

● Core cauliflower; steam for 10 to 15 minutes or until tender-crisp. Place in shallow bowl.

● In small bowl, whisk together vinegar, thyme, mustard, sugar, garlic, salt and pepper; gradually whisk in oil. Drizzle over cauliflower. Serve warm or at room temperature. Makes 4 to 6 servings.

TIP: For even cooking of a whole head of cauliflower, trim off all leaves and hollow out the stem right up into the head.

Maple Brussels Sprouts with Onions

A drizzle of maple syrup and slow-cooked caramelized onions combine with crisp cooked sprouts for a fall vegetable feast.

1 tbsp	vegetable oil	15 mL
1	large onion, halved and sliced	1
1-1/2 lb	brussels sprouts	750 g
2 tbsp	maple syrup	25 mL
	Salt and pepper	

● In large skillet, heat oil over medium-low heat; cook onion, stirring frequently, for about 20 minutes or until tender and golden.

● Add brussels sprouts and 1/4 cup (50 mL) water; increase heat to high, cover and cook for 5 minutes.

● Stir in maple syrup; cook, uncovered and stirring, for 5 to 10 minutes or until liquid has evaporated and brussels sprouts are tender and coated. Season with salt and pepper to taste. Makes 4 servings.

TIP: No maple syrup? Substitute 1 tbsp (15 mL) brown sugar.

CLOSE-UP ON BRUSSELS SPROUTS

Choose Well
● Choose tight bright green brussels sprouts. Small sprouts are superior to larger ones which are older and stronger flavored.

● Less compact sprouts have more wastage since outer leaves need to be removed.

● Avoid sprouts with yellow tinges. Select sprouts of uniform size for even cooking.

Quantity
● 1 lb (500 g) serves four.

Storage
● Store sprouts for up to a few days in the refrigerator, wrapped in toweling and enclosed in a plastic bag.

Preparation
● Trim off wilted or coarse outer leaves. Rinse sprouts.

● Cut thin end off stem and score a shallow X in bottom.

Cooking Basics
● Steam for 6 to 10 minutes, depending on size, or until tender with a slightly crunchy center. Or, boil, covered, in 2 inches (5 cm) boiling water for about 8 minutes.

● To preserve color, leave sprouts uncovered for first half of cooking time.

Nutrition Note
● Contribute beta carotene, thiamin, iron, fiber, potassium and phosphorus—and are very high in Vitamin C and folate.

Light and Creamy Spinach

1	pkg (10 oz/284 g) fresh spinach, trimmed	1
1 tbsp	butter	15 mL
1	clove garlic, minced	1
Pinch	cayenne	Pinch
	Salt and pepper	
1/4 cup	plain yogurt or light sour cream	50 mL
1/4 cup	pine nuts or slivered almonds, toasted	50 mL

● Rinse spinach; shake off excess water. In large pot, cover and cook spinach over medium heat, with just the water clinging to leaves, for 2 minutes or just until wilted. In sieve, drain well, gently pressing out moisture. Chop coarsely.

● In skillet, melt butter over medium-high heat; cook garlic, stirring, for 1 minute. Sprinkle with cayenne.

● Add spinach; cook for 2 to 3 minutes or until heated through. Season with salt and pepper to taste. Remove to warmed serving bowl. Stir in yogurt; sprinkle with pine nuts. Makes 3 servings.

Yogurt takes the place of cream in this easy and quick way to provide a nutritious vegetable that goes with any chicken or fish dish.

Spinach with Lemon and Nutmeg ▼

1	pkg (10 oz/284 g) fresh spinach, trimmed	1
2 tsp	lemon juice	10 mL
2 tsp	butter, melted	10 mL
Pinch	nutmeg	Pinch
	Salt and pepper	

● Rinse spinach; shake off excess water. In large pot, cover and cook spinach over medium heat, with just the water clinging to leaves, for 2 minutes or just until wilted. In sieve, drain well, gently pressing out moisture.

● Sprinkle with lemon juice, butter, nutmeg, and salt and pepper to taste. Makes 3 servings.

Quick cooking maximizes the nutrients you get from spinach. Lemon and nutmeg add the pizzazz.

FRESH OR FROZEN?
When time is short, substitute frozen spinach for fresh. One 10 oz (284 g) box yields about the same amount as a bag of the same weight fresh. Frozen spinach is a little "stemmier" than fresh, and the flavor's not quite as good, but it is close, and very convenient. Thaw and drain in a sieve, pressing out as much moisture as possible.

(from left) Spinach with Lemon and Nutmeg, potatoes and Sesame Carrots (p. 26)

CLOSE-UP ON SPINACH

Choose Well
● Bouncy dark-green crinkled leaf spinach is sold washed and bagged, and flatter spade-shaped leaf spinach is sold in bunches.

● Leaves should be crisp and deep green. Avoid bags with yellowed or translucent leaves.

Quantity
● 1 lb (500 g) leaf spinach or one 10 oz/284 g bag yields about 12 cups (3 mL) raw, 4 to 6 servings. Cooked, it yields 1 cup (250 mL), or 2 servings.

Storage
● Wrap bunch in toweling and enclose in plastic bag.

Preparation
● Wash in large sink of lukewarm water just before using. Remove spinach by handfuls; drain and repeat until no sand remains.

● Shake off excess moisture. Trim away coarse stems and ribs.

Cooking Basics
● In large pot, cover and cook spinach, with just the water clinging to leaves, over medium heat for about 2 minutes or until wilted. Drain in sieve, gently pressing out moisture.

Nutrition Note
● Very high in beta carotene and folate, and a good source of vitamin C, fiber, calcium and iron.

Sesame Spinach with Mushrooms

This delicious way to make spinach is perfect in an Asian menu, or with any summer grills, especially fish, chicken and chops.

1 tbsp	sesame seeds	15 mL
3 tbsp	vegetable oil	50 mL
2	large cloves garlic, minced	2
1/2 tsp	salt	2 mL
Pinch	pepper	Pinch
1	pkg (10 oz/284 g) fresh spinach, trimmed	1
1-1/2 cups	thinly sliced mushrooms (4 oz/125 g)	375 mL

● In wok or large skillet, toast sesame seeds over medium heat for 3 to 5 minutes or until golden brown. Set aside.

● Add 2 tbsp (25 mL) of the oil to wok; heat over high heat. Stir-fry garlic, salt and pepper for about 10 seconds or until fragrant. Add spinach; stir-fry for about 2 minutes or just until wilted. Remove to sieve. Drain well, gently pressing out moisture; keep warm.

● Drain and wipe wok dry; heat remaining oil. Stir-fry mushrooms for about 1 minute or just until limp. Add sesame seeds; remove from heat.

● Place spinach in warmed serving bowl; sprinkle with mushroom mixture. Makes 4 servings.

Fennel Gratin

An extravaganza reserved for connoisseurs who will appreciate every penny of the fennel! Serve with grilled fish, chicken, lamb or beef, or with crusty bread and sliced tomatoes for a vegetarian supper.

2	fennel bulbs	2
1 tbsp	lemon juice	15 mL
1/4 cup	freshly grated Parmesan cheese	50 mL
1/2 tsp	lemon rind	2 mL
1/4 tsp	pepper	1 mL

● Trim stalks from fennel bulbs; cut each bulb into quarters. Steam for about 20 minutes or until almost tender.

● Place, cut side up, in small shallow baking dish. Brush with lemon juice.

● Stir together Parmesan, lemon rind and pepper; sprinkle over fennel. Bake in 375°F (190°C) oven for 20 to 25 minutes or until tender and Parmesan is golden brown. Makes 4 servings.

Asparagus with Creamy Orange Vinaigrette

1 lb	asparagus spears, cooked	500 g
2 tbsp	chopped fresh chives or green onion	25 mL
	DRESSING	
1/2 cup	light mayonnaise	125 mL
1 tbsp	grated orange rind	15 mL
2 tbsp	orange juice	25 mL
1 tbsp	lemon juice	15 mL
1/2 tsp	Dijon mustard	2 mL
1/4 tsp	salt	1 mL
Pinch	pepper	Pinch

● DRESSING: In bowl, whisk together mayonnaise, orange rind and juice, lemon juice, mustard, salt and pepper.

● Arrange asparagus on serving platter; pour dressing over top. Sprinkle with chives. Makes 4 servings.

What could be simpler, or more delicious, than spring-green asparagus bathed in a pastel vinaigrette?

Skillet Asparagus with Mushrooms

12 oz	asparagus	375 g
1/4 cup	butter	50 mL
1 cup	small mushrooms	250 mL
2 tbsp	lemon juice	25 mL
1/4 tsp	dried tarragon	1 mL
	Salt and pepper	

● Trim asparagus; cut into 2-inch (5 cm) lengths. In large pot of boiling water, cook asparagus for 1 minute; drain and refresh under cold water. Drain again and pat dry.

● In large skillet, melt butter over medium heat; cook asparagus and mushrooms, stirring frequently, for about 5 minutes or until tender. Stir in lemon juice, tarragon, and salt and pepper to taste. Makes 2 servings.

You can blanch the asparagus ahead of time, wrap in towels, enclose in a plastic bag and refrigerate for up to 4 hours.

CLOSE-UP ON ASPARAGUS

Choose Well
● Choose straight, tall, firm green stalks (thin if preparing salads, thick for best flavor as a side dish) with tightly closed purple-tinged tips.

Quantity
● 1 lb (500 g) serves two generously and yields about 3 cups (750 mL) chopped.

Storage
● Remove any elastic bands or twist-ties; set in 1 inch (2.5 cm) water in pitcher and store in refrigerator. Or, wrap in towels, enclose in plastic bag and refrigerate for up to 2 days.

Preparation
● Holding asparagus by butt and halfway up stalk, snap off woody butt end, savings ends for soup. (If using for soup, pass soup through sieve to remove fibrous strands.)

● With thick stalks, trim butt ends with knife; using vegetable peeler, peel off skin thinly from the scales right down to the butt. Asparagus cooks slightly faster if peeled.

Cooking Basics
● In a wide skillet of boiling water, or sitting upright in a tall asparagus cooker or top of double boiler, cook asparagus, covered, for about 5 minutes per lb (500 g). Or, steam for about 7 minutes.

Nutrition Note
● A good source of beta carotene and vitamin C, with a fair amount of iron.

CLOSE-UP ON BEANS

Choose Well
● Fresh beans should be slim, crisp, brightly colored (green, yellow or purple) and free of blemishes.

● Bypass shrivelled or leathery beans and mature swollen beans.

Quantity
● 1 lb (500 g) yields about 4 cups (1 L) in 1-inch (2.5 cm) pieces and serves four.

Storage
● Wrap, unwashed, in toweling; store in plastic bag in crisper for up to 3 days.

Preparation
● Cut off stem end; rinse. Tender beans don't need to be cut on diagonal.

Cooking Basics
● Cook, covered, in 1 inch (2.5 cm) boiling water for 3 to 6 minutes or until tender-

crisp. Or, steam for about 10 minutes.

Nutrition Note
● A source of vitamins A and C, potassium, folate and fiber.

Green Beans Gremolata

1 lb	green beans, trimmed	500 g
1 tbsp	chopped fresh parsley	15 mL
2 tsp	grated lemon rind	10 mL
1	clove garlic, minced	1
1 tsp	extra virgin olive oil	5 mL
	Salt and pepper	

● In large pot of lightly salted boiling water, cook beans for 5 minutes or until tender-crisp; drain well.

● Combine parsley, lemon rind and garlic; toss with beans along with oil. Season with salt and pepper to taste. Makes 4 servings.

Grated lemon rind, garlic and parsley jazz up green beans as well as new potatoes, carrots, baby zucchini and broccoli.

Stir-Fried Green Beans and Sweet Peppers

1 lb	green beans, trimmed	500 g
1/4 cup	cold water	50 mL
1 tbsp	soy sauce	15 mL
1 tsp	cornstarch	5 mL
1 tbsp	peanut or vegetable oil	15 mL
Half	each sweet red and yellow pepper, cut into strips	Half
1	clove garlic, minced	1

● In large pot of boiling salted water, cook beans for 3 minutes; drain and refresh under cold water. Pat dry.

● Stir together cold water, soy sauce and cornstarch; set aside.

● In wok or large skillet, heat oil over high heat; stir-fry beans, red and yellow peppers and garlic for 2 to 3 minutes or until beans are tender. Stir cornstarch mixture and add to wok; cook, stirring, for 1 minute or until thickened. Makes 4 servings.

Summer's the best time to marry crisp emerald-green beans and vibrant red and yellow peppers in a pleaser of a dish. Serve with grilled or steamed fish accented with ginger.

Green Beans with Asian Flair

1 lb	green beans, trimmed	500 g
2 tbsp	sesame seeds	25 mL
1 tbsp	mirin (rice wine)	15 mL
2 tsp	soy sauce	10 mL
1 tsp	sesame oil	5 mL
	Salt and pepper	

● In large pot of lightly salted boiling water, cook beans for 5 minutes or until tender-crisp; drain well.

● Meanwhile, in small skillet, toast sesame seeds over medium-high heat, stirring often, for 2 to 3 minutes or until golden.

● Combine mirin, soy sauce and sesame oil; toss with beans. Season with salt and pepper to taste. Sprinkle with sesame seeds. Makes 4 servings.

Here's a delicious and sophisticated new take on ever-popular, always available green beans.

Potatoes Anna ◀

1/2 cup	butter	125 mL
2	large sweet potatoes	2
2	large baking potatoes	2
1 tsp	pepper	5 mL
1/2 tsp	salt	2 mL
1/2 tsp	dried thyme or oregano	2 mL
1 tbsp	chopped fresh parsley	15 mL

● In small saucepan, melt butter over low heat; let stand for 2 to 3 minutes or until foam rises to top. Skim off foam.

● Peel sweet potatoes; cut into thin slices. Spread on paper towels to remove excess moisture. Repeat with baking potatoes.

● Brush 10-inch (25 cm) nonstick ovenproof skillet with a little of the butter. Arrange one-quarter of the baking potatoes in overlapping circles in pan. Brush with enough of the butter to coat. Combine pepper, salt and thyme; sprinkle some lightly over potatoes.

● Repeat with one-third of the sweet potatoes; sprinkle with some of the pepper mixture. Repeat layering twice. Arrange remaining baking potatoes over top, pressing down gently.

● Cook over medium-high heat for 10 minutes or until bottom is browned. Cover and bake in 450°F (230°C) oven for 10 minutes; uncover and bake for 15 minutes or until potatoes are tender and top is light brown. Broil for 1 to 2 minutes or until crisp.

● Spoon off any excess butter. Let stand for 5 minutes. Sprinkle with parsley. To serve, cut into wedges. Or, loosen edges and bottom and carefully slide onto warmed serving platter. Makes 6 servings.

If mashed potatoes says everyday, Potatoes Anna says company. Thinly sliced, intermingled with sweet potatoes and arranged in overlapping circles, the potatoes crisp and gild to elegant perfection.

CLOSE-UP ON SWEET POTATOES

Choose Well
● Choose firm, smooth-skinned sweet potatoes. Avoid ones with soft spots and shrivelled ends.

Quantity
● Three average sweet potatoes total 1 lb (500 g) and serve three. Mashed, these potatoes yield about 2-1/2 cups (625 mL).

Storage
● Store at room temperature for up to 1 week, or in the refrigerator for a few weeks longer.

Preparation
● Scrub well. Trim ends and leave skin on for baking or microwaving whole.

● Peel only if boiling or steaming.

Cooking Basics
● To bake, prick in several places; bake in 400°F (200°C) oven for about 45 minutes or until skin is crisp and potato is soft when pressed.

● Boil halves in water, covered, for about 20 minutes or until tender, or steam halves for about 30 minutes.

Nutrition Note
● Extremely high in beta carotene, and an excellent source of vitamin C, potassium and fiber.

Keep in Mind
● The vegetables sold in North America as either sweet potatoes or yams are really all sweet potatoes, although the flesh can range from yellow to a deep orange, their shape either rounded or long and pointed.

● True yams are a pale cream color and can weigh up to 100 lb (45 kg). They grow in the tropics and are sold in Caribbean groceries.

Herbed Potato Casserole

This scalloped potato dish is made creamier, more convenient and tastier with a quick sauce made from herbed cream cheese melted with milk.

8 oz	herbed cream cheese, cubed	250 g
2 cups	milk	500 mL
5	large potatoes, peeled	5
1/2 tsp	each salt and pepper	2 mL
2 tbsp	freshly grated Parmesan cheese	25 mL
4 tsp	butter, in bits	20 mL

● In saucepan, stir together cream cheese and milk over medium heat for about 5 minutes or just until smooth. Remove from heat.

● Slice potatoes thinly; arrange in overlapping layers in greased 11 - x 7-inch (2 L) baking dish, sprinkling with salt and pepper. Pour milk mixture over top. Sprinkle with Parmesan; dot with butter.

● Bake in 400°F (200°C) oven for 50 to 55 minutes or until tender. Let stand for 10 minutes before serving. Makes 8 servings.

Skinny Buttermilk Mashed Potatoes

If you think that really good mashed potatoes can only be made with cream and loads of butter, this lower-fat buttermilk version will definitely make you change your mind!

6	potatoes, peeled	6
1-1/4 cups	buttermilk	300 mL
1 tbsp	butter	15 mL
1 tbsp	chopped fresh dill	15 mL
1 tbsp	chopped fresh chives or green onion tops	15 mL
	Salt and pepper	

● In pot of boiling salted water, cook potatoes for about 20 minutes or until fork-tender; drain well. Mash, rice or pass potatoes through food mill to remove all lumps.

● Using fork, gradually beat in buttermilk, then butter. Stir in dill and chives. Season with salt and pepper to taste. *(Potatoes can be covered and refrigerated for up to 1 day; reheat in microwave at High for 5 minutes, rotating twice.)* Makes 8 servings.

The Very Best Home Fries

A good well-seasoned cast-iron frying pan makes superior home fries, but a nonstick skillet will still get you the golden crusty bits and steaming chunky potatoes that are so wonderful with eggs and peameal bacon.

4	large potatoes	4
2 tbsp	vegetable oil	25 mL
1 tbsp	butter	15 mL
1	green onion, sliced	1
1	clove garlic, minced	1
1/4 tsp	salt	1 mL
Pinch	each pepper and paprika	Pinch

● Scrub potatoes. In pot of boiling salted water, cook potatoes for 15 minutes or until tender but firm; drain well. Refrigerate until cold. Cut into 1/2-inch (1 cm) cubes.

● In nonstick skillet, heat oil and butter over high heat; cook potatoes, turning to coat all over, for 3 to 4 minutes.

● Cook for about 8 minutes longer, turning often, or until crisp and golden. Remove from heat; stir in onion, garlic, salt, pepper and paprika. Makes 4 servings.

Fried Red Tomatoes

1 cup	cornmeal	250 mL
1 tsp	crushed fennel seeds	5 mL
1 tsp	dried oregano	5 mL
3/4 tsp	salt	4 mL
1/2 tsp	cayenne pepper	2 mL
1/4 tsp	pepper	1 mL
2	eggs	2
2 tbsp	water	25 mL
4	beefsteak tomatoes	4
1/2 cup	all-purpose flour	125 mL
2 tbsp	olive oil	25 mL
2 tbsp	butter	25 mL

● In shallow dish, combine cornmeal, fennel seeds, oregano, salt, cayenne and pepper. In another dish, beat eggs with water.

● Cut thin slice from top and bottom of each tomato; cut each tomato into 3 thick slices. Dip each slice into flour to coat; shake off excess. Dip into egg mixture; dip into cornmeal mixture, pressing mixture on to coat.

● In skillet, heat half of the oil and butter over medium-high heat; add half of the tomatoes and reduce heat to medium. Cook, gently turning once, for 5 to 7 minutes or until golden. Repeat with remaining oil, butter and tomatoes. Makes 4 servings.

TIP: Bread the tomatoes just before cooking.

Enjoy crunchy tomato slices with eggs for breakfast or brunch, with cold meat for light suppers, or with chicken or chops off the grill.

Warmed Tomatoes with Basil and Brie

4	large tomatoes	4
2 tbsp	olive oil	25 mL
6	large basil leaves, shredded	6
8 oz	Brie cheese	250 g

● Core and cut tomatoes into thick slices; arrange on ovenproof platter. Drizzle with oil; sprinkle with basil.

● Remove rind from Brie. Chop cheese and scatter over tomatoes. *(Tomatoes can be prepared to this point and set aside for up to 1 hour.)* Broil for 1 to 2 minutes or just until cheese has melted. Makes 6 servings.

Chunks of Brie melt and ooze over thick tomato slices and peppery fresh basil. Summer lunch has never been easier — or more luscious! Crusty sourdough bread is perfect for mopping up every last juicy bit.

Mustard Mayo-Glazed Tomato Slices

2	large tomatoes	2
2 tbsp	freshly grated Parmesan cheese	25 mL
2 tbsp	light mayonnaise	25 mL
1 tbsp	chopped fresh parsley	15 mL
1 tbsp	chopped green onion	15 mL
1 tsp	Dijon mustard	5 mL
1/4 tsp	dried oregano	1 mL
1/4 tsp	each salt and pepper	1 mL

● Core and cut each tomato into 3 thick slices; arrange in shallow greased baking dish.

● Stir together Parmesan, mayonnaise, parsley, onion, mustard, oregano, salt and pepper; spread over tomatoes. Bake in 400°F (200°C) oven for about 12 minutes or until tender. Makes 4 servings.

With more pizzazz than plain tomatoes, and less work than a casserole, these slices of summer add a juicy touch to no-fuss brunches or suppers.

Soups and Starters

Showcase vegetables in soups — elegant and inexpensive dinner party openers or hearty Saturday simmers — and let them provide the sparkle in an impressive array of appetizers and snacks.

Fresh and Spicy Squash Soup ▶

Fresh ginger and coriander give a fall classic a total taste make-over. This soup is adult dinner fare and will set taste buds tingling for the rest of the evening.

2 tbsp	vegetable oil	25 mL
2	onions, chopped	2
1	clove garlic, chopped	1
1	stalk celery, chopped	1
1/4 cup	minced gingerroot	50 mL
1/4 cup	chopped fresh coriander	50 mL
2 tsp	ground coriander seeds	10 mL
1 tsp	ground cumin	5 mL
1/2 tsp	each salt and pepper	2 mL
1/4 tsp	grated lemon rind	1 mL
1/4 tsp	turmeric	1 mL
1/4 tsp	hot pepper flakes	1 mL
8 cups	cubed peeled butternut squash (3 lb/1.5 kg)	2 L
1	tomato, chopped	1
4 cups	chicken or vegetable stock	1 L
1	can (400 mL) coconut milk	1
1/2 cup	fresh coriander leaves	125 mL

● In large heavy saucepan or Dutch oven, heat oil over medium heat; cook onions, garlic, celery, ginger, chopped fresh coriander and ground seeds, cumin, salt, pepper, lemon rind, turmeric and hot pepper flakes, stirring, for 5 to 8 minutes or until aromatic and onions are softened.

● Stir in squash and tomato; pour in stock and bring to boil. Reduce heat to low; cover and simmer for about 20 minutes or until squash is tender.

● In blender or food processor, purée soup, in batches, until smooth. Return to clean saucepan; reheat until steaming. Stir in coconut milk; heat through. Serve sprinkled with coriander leaves. Makes 8 servings.

HERB GARNISHES

With fresh herbs and a little imagination, it's easy to dress up a simple bowl of soup.

● Instead of the usual sprig of parsley, chop parsley finely and dust it lightly over the soup and wide rim of bowl.

Do the same with other fresh herbs such as coriander, dill, chives, basil and chervil.
● Create a design with herbs. Out of the center of a piece

of cardboard, cut a shape, initial or number, depending on the occasion. Hold cutout just above the soup bowl and

sprinkle finely chopped parsley or other herb through it to create a pattern on the soup.
● See Soup Toppers, p. 61, for other eye-appealing ideas.

Three Sisters Soup

From the kitchen of chef Bertha Skye comes this traditional Iroquois soup made with squash, beans and corn — the "three sisters" of Iroquois agriculture and cooking. Delicately flavored and colorful, the soup won chef Skye a gold medal at the 1992 Culinary Olympics in Frankfurt.

2 cups	corn kernels	500 mL
2 cups	chopped green beans	500 mL
2 cups	cubed peeled butternut squash	500 mL
1-1/2 cups	diced peeled potatoes	375 mL
2 tbsp	all-purpose flour	25 mL
2 tbsp	butter, softened	25 mL
3/4 tsp	salt	4 mL
1/2 tsp	pepper	2 mL

● In large pot, bring corn, green beans, squash, potatoes and 5 cups (1.25 L) water to boil. Reduce heat; cover and simmer for about 10 minutes or until vegetables are almost tender.

● Blend flour with butter; stir into soup. Increase heat to medium; cook, stirring occasionally, for about 5 minutes or until thickened slightly and vegetables are tender. Stir in salt and pepper. Makes 4 to 6 servings.

CLOSE-UP ON CORN

Choose Well
● Choose cobs that have dark, stiff, moist silk and moist bright green husks that completely cover the ear.

● Individual corn kernels should be mature enough to be felt through the husk.

● Buy corn as fresh as possible. It's best if eaten within a few hours.

Quantity
● One large cob should be enough per serving.

Storage
● Wrap unhusked corn in toweling and enclose in plastic bag; store for up to 2 days in refrigerator.

Preparation
● Just before cooking, husk cobs and pick off any silk sticking to the kernels.

● If barbecuing, peel back husks partway and remove silk. Close husks, secure with string at top and soak in cold water for 20 minutes.

Cooking Basics
● To boil, place cobs in large pot of boiling water; boil for 3 to 5 minutes or until kernels are tender when pierced. Do not add salt to water as it toughens the kernels.

● To barbecue, place on grill over medium-high heat; close cover and cook, turning frequently, for about 20 minutes or until husks are charred and corn is deep yellow.

Nutrition Note
● Corn, especially yellow corn, contributes folate and fiber to the diet.

Keep in Mind
● There are three different classes of sweet corn. Within each group are yellow, white and bicolor types.

● Normal sweet corn has the most tender kernels and a sugar content of 9 to 16 per cent. This corn must be eaten as soon as possible after picking as sugar turns quickly into starch.

Corn Soup with Red Pepper Swirl

1 tbsp	butter	15 mL
2	onions, chopped	2
1	clove garlic, minced	1
3/4 tsp	crumbled dried sage	4 mL
4 cups	corn kernels	1 L
2 tbsp	all-purpose flour	25 mL
1-1/2 cups	chicken stock	375 mL
1 cup	milk	250 mL
1/2 tsp	salt	2 mL
	RED PEPPER SAUCE	
1	sweet red pepper, roasted, peeled and seeded (see p. 89)	1
2 tbsp	milk	25 mL
1 tsp	minced jalapeño pepper (or pinch cayenne)	5 mL
1/2 tsp	each salt and pepper	2 mL

● In saucepan, melt butter over medium heat. Add onions, garlic and sage; cover and cook, stirring occasionally, for 3 minutes or until softened. Stir in corn; cook, stirring, for 5 minutes. Remove 1 cup (250 mL); set aside.

● Stir in flour to coat vegetables; cook for 1 minute. Pour in stock and bring to boil, stirring frequently; reduce heat to low and simmer for about 5 minutes or until thickened.

● In food processor or blender, purée soup, in batches if necessary, until smooth; return to saucepan. Stir in reserved corn mixture, milk and salt; heat through but do not boil.

● RED PEPPER SAUCE: Meanwhile, in blender, purée together red pepper, milk, jalapeño pepper, salt and pepper.

● Using spoon, attractively swirl about 2 tbsp (25 mL) sauce into each bowl of soup (see Soup Toppers, p. 61). Makes 4 servings.

Plain soups are OK for busy days, but when there's time to fuss a little, a swirl of a contrasting vegetable purée jazzes up an easy soup with extra flavor and appeal. Choose the freshest, deepest yellow corn to give this late-summer soup maximum color contrast.

TIP: When sweet red peppers are prohibitively expensive, try the roasted ones in jars. They are less work, taste just fine and add lots of color not only to this soup, but also to dips, salads and pasta dishes.

15-Minute Tomato Soup For Two

2 tsp	olive oil	10 mL
1	small onion, chopped	1
1	small zucchini, diced	1
1	tomato, peeled and diced	1
1 cup	tomato juice	250 mL
1 cup	chicken or vegetable stock	250 mL
1/2 tsp	granulated sugar	2 mL
1/4 tsp	each dried oregano and basil	1 mL
1/2 cup	corn kernels	125 mL
	Salt and pepper	

● In saucepan, heat oil over medium heat; cook onion and zucchini, stirring occasionally, for 3 minutes.

● Add tomato, tomato juice, chicken stock, sugar, oregano and basil; bring to boil. Reduce heat and simmer for 5 minutes.

● Add corn; simmer for 2 to 4 minutes or until heated through. Season with salt and pepper to taste. Makes 2 servings.

Almost as fast as opening a can, homemade tomato soup is ideal for the Thermos or a quick weekend lunch. To serve four, simply double the recipe.

Tomato Bread Soup ▲

In Italy, bread is usually bought fresh daily since it is made with little or no fat and dries out quickly. This cubed bread and tomato soup is just one of the thrifty and delicious ways Italians have of using up their bread while celebrating the ripest, reddest and most sun-sopped tomatoes of the harvest.

1 tbsp	olive oil	15 mL
1	small leek (white part only), chopped	1
4	cloves garlic, minced	4
2 cups	chopped peeled tomatoes (1 lb/500 g)	500 mL
1/3 cup	chopped fresh basil	75 mL
1-1/2 cups	(approx) vegetable or chicken stock	375 mL
1/2 tsp	each salt and pepper	2 mL
2 cups	day-old cubed Italian bread	500 mL
2 tbsp	freshly grated Parmesan cheese	25 mL

● In heavy saucepan, heat oil over medium heat; cook leek and garlic, stirring occasionally, for 3 minutes or until softened.

● Stir in tomatoes and basil; bring to boil. Boil gently for 5 to 10 minutes or until slightly thickened.

● Add 1 cup (250 mL) of the stock, salt and pepper; bring to boil, stirring. Remove from heat; stir in bread. If necessary, warm remaining stock and add enough to reach desired consistency. Serve sprinkled with Parmesan. Makes 2 servings.

TIP: To peel tomatoes, plunge into boiling water for 30 to 60 seconds or until skins loosen. Chill in cold water, drain and peel.

Celery Root Soup with Parsnip Chips

2	sprigs each fresh parsley and thyme	2
2	bay leaves	2
2 tbsp	butter	25 mL
1 cup	chopped leeks (white part only)	250 mL
1 cup	sliced celery	250 mL
1 cup	sliced fennel	250 mL
1 lb	celery root or Jerusalem artichokes	500 g
4 cups	(approx) chicken stock	1 L
	Salt and pepper	
	PARSNIP CHIPS	
1	parsnip	1
1/3 cup	peanut oil	75 mL

● In double-thickness square of cheesecloth, tie together parsley, thyme and bay leaves; set aside.

● In large saucepan, melt butter over medium heat; cook leeks, celery and fennel, stirring often, for 5 minutes.

● Meanwhile, peel and thinly slice celery root; add to pan along with chicken stock and bag of herbs. Bring to boil; reduce heat and simmer for 25 minutes or until celery root is tender. Discard herbs.

● In blender, purée soup, in batches if necessary, until smooth, adding up to 1/2 cup (125 mL) more stock if soup is too thick. Season with salt and pepper to taste.

● PARSNIP CHIPS: Meanwhile, peel parsnip; using vegetable peeler, peel into thin strips. In deep skillet, heat oil over high heat; deep-fry parsnip, in batches, for 2 to 3 minutes or until golden. With slotted spoon, remove and drain on paper towels. Scatter over each bowl of soup. Makes 4 servings.

At the first Northern Bounty conference held in Stratford, Ontario, chef Neil Baxter of Rundles Restaurant created this soup, a bowlful to rave about even without the parsnip chips. Knobbly and dark brown with many rootlets, celery root won't win any beauty contests, but it sure is delicious in this soup, or grated into salads or cooked and mashed with potatoes.

Parsnip and Cheddar Soup

1/4 cup	butter	50 mL
1-1/2 cups	chopped onions	375 mL
3-1/2 cups	diced peeled parsnips (about 1 lb/500 g)	875 mL
1/4 tsp	ground cumin	1 mL
1-1/2 cups	water	375 mL
1/2 tsp	salt	2 mL
1/4 tsp	pepper	1 mL
4 cups	milk	1 L
2 cups	shredded old Cheddar cheese	500 mL

● In large heavy saucepan, melt butter over low heat; cover and cook onions, stirring occasionally, for about 5 minutes or until softened.

● Add parsnips and cumin; cook, covered, for 8 minutes or until parsnips are softened. Add water, salt and pepper; cook, covered, for 30 minutes or until parsnips are tender.

● In food processor or blender, purée soup, in batches if necessary, until smooth.

● Return soup to saucepan. Stir in milk; cook over low heat just until heated through. Remove from heat; stir in Cheddar until blended. Makes 6 servings.

This hearty cold-weather soup comes from Say Cheese, a very fine cheese shop and restaurant in London, Ontario. It's especially delicious sprinkled with Garlic Popcorn (below).

GARLIC POPCORN
In small saucepan, melt 2 tbsp (25 mL) butter over medium-low heat; cook 1 minced clove garlic until softened. Drizzle over 9 cups (2.25 L) popped corn; season with salt to taste. Toss well. Makes 9 cups (2.25 L).

Pesto Cucumber Gazpacho

*Nothing is more cooling —
both for the cook and the
consumer! — than a cold
cucumber soup. This new
version gets its pep from
pesto, either make-your-own,
or store-bought if you're short
of time.*

2	English cucumbers	2
1	tomato, seeded	1
1 cup	Pesto (recipe follows)	250 mL
2 tbsp	red wine vinegar	25 mL
1/2 tsp	each salt and pepper	2 mL

● Chop cucumbers and tomato into chunks; place in blender. Add pesto, vinegar, salt and pepper; purée until smooth. Makes 6 servings.

	PESTO	
1 cup	lightly packed fresh basil leaves	250 mL
1/2 cup	pine nuts	125 mL
1/3 cup	freshly grated Parmesan cheese	75 mL
1/4 cup	lemon juice	50 mL
1/2 cup	extra virgin olive oil	125 mL
2	cloves garlic, minced	2
1/4 tsp	each salt and pepper	1 mL

● In blender or food processor, finely chop together basil, pine nuts, Parmesan and lemon juice. With motor running, gradually drizzle in oil until well combined. Stir in garlic, salt and pepper. Makes 1 cup (250 mL).

Leek and Potato Soup

*Hot, this light version of
vichyssoise warms right to the
toes. Cold, it's always a chic
starter for summer get-
togethers. For a vegetarian
version, simply replace the
chicken stock with vegetable
stock (see box, below).*

4	large leeks	4
2 tbsp	butter	25 mL
2	potatoes, peeled and cubed	2
1	onion, chopped	1
4 cups	chicken stock	1 L
1 cup	milk	250 mL
	Salt and pepper	
2 tbsp	light cream	25 mL
1/4 cup	chopped fresh chives	50 mL

● Trim outer leaves and dark green tops from leeks; cut lengthwise in half almost all the way through, leaving root end intact. Spread leaves and rinse in cold water; shake off water and chop to make about 4 cups (1 L).

● In large heavy saucepan, melt butter over low heat. Add leeks, potatoes and onion; cover and cook, stirring occasionally, for 15 minutes or until softened. Add stock; simmer gently, covered, for about 20 minutes or until vegetables are tender.

● In blender or food processor, purée soup, in batches if necessary, until smooth. Return to saucepan; add milk and heat through. Season with salt and pepper to taste. Serve hot or chilled, garnished with a swirl of cream and sprinkle of chives. Makes 8 servings.

VEGETABLE STOCK

In a pinch, vegetable stock can simply be the water saved from boiling vegetables such as carrots and potatoes. At the convenience end of the spectrum, frozen vegetable stock is available in some specialty stores, and makers of stock cubes and powders have produced a vegetable version to go with their chicken and beef. To make your own, see recipe on p. 61.

Creamed Carrot Soup with Coriander ▲

2 tbsp	butter	25 mL
1	onion, chopped	1
12	carrots, chopped	12
1/4 cup	all-purpose flour	50 mL
3 cups	chicken stock	750 mL
1	bay leaf	1
3 tbsp	chopped fresh coriander or parsley	50 mL
2 cups	milk	500 mL
1 tsp	salt	5 mL
1/2 tsp	pepper	2 mL

● In heavy saucepan, melt butter over medium heat; cook onion for about 5 minutes or until softened. Add carrots; cook, covered, for about 15 minutes or until softened. Sprinkle flour over carrot mixture; stir until well blended.

● In measuring cup, combine stock with 3 cups (750 mL) water. Stir into saucepan along with bay leaf and 2 tbsp (25 mL) coriander; cook for 15 to 20 minutes or until carrots are tender. Remove bay leaf and discard.

● In blender or food processor, purée mixture until smooth. Return to saucepan; stir in milk, salt and pepper. Cook over low heat just until heated through. Garnish with remaining coriander. Makes 6 to 8 servings.

Carrots dress up for dinner in this easy yet elegant soup. Add a little drama to the presentation by serving in black and gold soup bowls, as we did for our photograph.

Cream of Fiddlehead Soup

Whether you pick your own edible ferns, buy them fresh at the market or can only find them in the frozen food section of the supermarket, you'll enjoy their delicate flavor in this classic soup from New Brunswick.

1/4 cup	butter	50 mL
1 cup	sliced leeks or onions	250 mL
2 tbsp	all-purpose flour	25 mL
2-1/2 cups	chicken stock	625 mL
4 cups	fresh fiddleheads	1 L
2 cups	light cream	500 mL
1 tbsp	lemon juice	15 mL
1/4 tsp	pepper	1 mL
Pinch	cayenne pepper	Pinch
	Salt	
1/4 cup	sour cream	50 mL

● In large saucepan, melt butter over low heat; cover and cook leeks, stirring often, for 10 to 15 minutes or until softened but not browned. Sprinkle with flour; cook, stirring, for 2 minutes. Gradually stir in stock; bring to boil over medium-high heat, stirring constantly.

● Add fiddleheads and return to boil; reduce heat to medium, cover and simmer for 5 to 6 minutes or until fiddleheads are tender.

● Remove 6 fiddleheads and set aside for garnish. In blender or food processor, purée soup, in batches if necessary, until smooth.

● Return soup to saucepan. Stir in cream; heat through over medium heat, stirring often and being careful not to boil. Stir in lemon juice, pepper, cayenne, and salt to taste. Serve garnished with sour cream and reserved fiddleheads. Makes 6 servings.

TIP: If using frozen fiddleheads, thaw and drain before adding to soup.

Cheddar Carrot Soup

Milk, not cream, delivers all the smooth and satisfying richness of this glorious orange soup — and that's delicious news if you're looking for something creamy but light.

1 tbsp	vegetable oil	15 mL
1	onion, chopped	1
6	carrots, chopped	6
5 cups	chicken stock	1.25 L
2 tbsp	rice	25 mL
1 tsp	Worcestershire sauce	5 mL
1/4 tsp	dried thyme	1 mL
1	bay leaf	1
Dash	hot pepper sauce	Dash
Pinch	pepper	Pinch
1-1/2 cups	milk	375 mL
1 cup	shredded old Cheddar cheese	250 mL
	Salt	

● In large saucepan, heat oil over medium heat; cook onion, stirring occasionally, for 5 minutes or until softened.

● Add carrots, stock, rice, Worcestershire sauce, thyme, bay leaf, hot pepper sauce and pepper; bring to boil. Reduce heat to low; simmer for 25 minutes or until carrots are tender. Discard bay leaf.

● In blender or food processor, purée soup, in batches if necessary, until smooth. Return to saucepan; stir in milk. *(Soup can be prepared to this point and refrigerated in airtight container for up to 1 day or frozen for up to 2 weeks.)*

● Bring to simmer. Stir in Cheddar; cook, stirring, over low heat until melted. Season with salt to taste. Makes 4 servings.

Bowl-of-Jewels Borscht

1 tbsp	vegetable oil	15 mL
1	large onion, chopped	1
1	large carrot, chopped	1
2	stalks celery, chopped	2
1	bay leaf	1
Pinch	caraway seeds	Pinch
4	beets (with leaves)	4
2	large red-skinned potatoes	2
4 cups	beef, chicken or vegetable stock	1 L
1	can (19 oz/540 mL) tomatoes, chopped	1
4 tsp	vinegar	20 mL
	Salt and pepper	
1/4 cup	light sour cream	50 mL
2 tbsp	chopped fresh dill	25 mL

● In large heavy saucepan or Dutch oven, heat oil over medium heat; cook onion, carrot, celery, bay leaf and caraway seeds, stirring often, for about 15 minutes or until onions are softened.

● Meanwhile, trim stalks from beets. Coarsely chop enough of the leaves to make 2 cups (500 mL); set aside. Peel and cube beets. Peel potatoes if desired and cube.

● Add beets, potatoes and stock to pan; bring to boil. Cover and reduce heat; simmer for about 20 minutes or until vegetables are tender. Add tomatoes; cook for 20 minutes.

● Stir in reserved beet greens; cook for about 2 minutes or until tender. Add vinegar; season with salt and pepper to taste. Discard bay leaf. Serve dolloped with sour cream and sprinkled with dill. Makes 4 to 6 servings.

TIP: When beets with tops are not available, substitute the same amount of shredded cabbage or Swiss chard for beet greens.

If you don't have a Baba in your family, this recipe will make up for it! (Photo, p. 4)

Curried Zucchini Soup

1 tbsp	vegetable oil	15 mL
5 cups	chopped zucchini (about 6 small)	1.25 L
2	onions, chopped	2
1	stalk celery, diced	1
1	clove garlic, minced	1
2 tsp	curry powder	10 mL
3/4 tsp	(approx) salt	4 mL
1/2 tsp	cinnamon	2 mL
1/4 tsp	(approx) pepper	1 mL
1 tsp	packed brown sugar	5 mL
6 cups	vegetable stock or water	1.5 L

● In large saucepan, heat oil over medium heat; cook zucchini, onions, celery, garlic, curry powder, salt, cinnamon and pepper, stirring occasionally, for 10 minutes or until softened.

● Sprinkle with sugar; pour in stock and bring to boil. Reduce heat to medium; simmer, covered, for 20 minutes or until vegetables are very tender.

● In blender, purée zucchini mixture, in batches, until smooth. Pour into clean saucepan; reheat but do not boil. Season with more salt and pepper to taste. Makes 8 servings.

A wisp of curry magnifies the appeal of plentiful summer zucchini. For extra flavor, top with a dollop of yogurt and a spoonful of chutney.

Light and Creamy Broccoli Soup ▲

To take the "cream" out of "creamy" in this lightened-up version of a popular soup, simmer a potato along with the broccoli. Then, simply purée — the potato adds body without fat and all the nutrients in the liquid stay in the soup.

1	bunch broccoli	1
1	onion, chopped	1
2 cups	diced peeled potatoes	500 mL
1	clove garlic, minced	1
1-1/2 cups	vegetable stock or water	375 mL
1/2 tsp	dried thyme	2 mL
1/4 tsp	pepper	1 mL
Pinch	nutmeg	Pinch
1-1/2 cups	milk	375 mL
	Salt	

● Separate broccoli into florets; set 2 cups (500 mL) aside for garnish. Peel stems; chop coarsely.

● In saucepan, combine stems and remaining florets, onion, potatoes, garlic, stock, thyme, pepper and nutmeg; bring to boil. Reduce heat, cover and simmer for 10 minutes or until potatoes are tender.

● Meanwhile, steam reserved florets for 5 minutes or until tender.

● In blender or food processor, purée soup, in batches if necessary, until smooth; return to saucepan. Add milk; heat through without boiling. Season with salt to taste. Divide florets among soup bowls; pour soup over top. Makes 5 servings.

Roasted Vegetable Stock

3	carrots	3
3	onions (unpeeled)	3
3	stalks celery	3
3	tomatoes (or 1 can 19 oz/540 mL, drained)	3
2 tsp	vegetable oil	10 mL
8 cups	water	2 L
2	cloves garlic	2
1/3 cup	parsley stems	75 mL
2	bay leaves	2
12	peppercorns	12

● Scrub carrots. Cut carrots, onions, celery and tomatoes into chunks; place in roasting pan. Add oil, stirring to coat vegetables. Roast in 450°F (230°C) oven for 20 minutes or until browned.

● In stockpot, combine roasted vegetables, water, garlic, parsley, bay leaves and peppercorns. Bring to boil; skim off foam. Reduce heat to medium; simmer for 35 to 40 minutes or until well flavored. Strain. Makes about 6 cups (1.5 L).

TIP: Always simmer stock uncovered to concentrate the flavors.

When vegetable stock is called for, this roasted vegetable medley delivers a deep rich flavor that will enhance any dish.

SENSATIONAL SOUP TOPPERS

Crunchy Toppings
● Why settle for soda crackers in your bowl of soup when you can spoon on the crunch of your choice — crushed potato chips, nacho chips, sliced almonds, seasoned croutons, crisp chow mein noodles or garlic popcorn (recipe, p. 55).

Bread
● Top bowls of hearty soup with Italian or other crusty bread you've rubbed with garlic, brushed with olive oil and toasted golden crisp.
● For hearty appetites, sprinkle the toasted bread with shredded cheese and run the bowls under the broiler. Just be sure the bowls are heatproof.

Vegetables
● Go fresh with chopped vegetables that complement the soup with color and crunch. Tomatoes, cucumber, green and red onions, radishes and celery are good choices.
● Lay 2 or 3 stalks of chives over a thick soup.
● For soups made from asparagus, broccoli, peas, fiddleheads or other green vegetables, blanch a few uncooked vegetables until tender-crisp to garnish soup.
● Shred or shave carrots and sprinkle over soups.

Flowers
● Garnish soup with home-grown unsprayed edible flowers such as nasturtium (flowers and leaves), chive blossoms (pulled apart and scattered artfully over a bowl of soup) or calendula marigold petals.

Swirls
● Puréed sweet red or yellow pepper works best for adding a swirl of color and taste. Thick yogurt and sour cream are good, too.
● Spoon a dollop of yogurt or purée onto center of soup in bowl, then dip the narrow tip of a knife into the dollop and pull it lightly back out to form a light-colored streak in the contrasting soup. Repeat around the dollop until you have a star.
● Or, place yogurt or other swirlable purée or sauce in a clean mustard squirt bottle and zigzag or swirl across the soup.

Cheese
● Sprinkle soup with shredded Asiago, provolone, Gruyère or old Cheddar, cubed Brie, or use a vegetable peeler to shave Parmesan over the surface.
● For younger taste buds, choose a milder cheese such as Gouda, Swiss or Monterey Jack. For lighter taste buds, try Danbo or low-fat versions of Cheddar.

A Trio of Summer Dips

*Dip into casual warm-weather entertaining with three classic Greek dips — a smooth hummus
with the earthiness of tahini and cumin, a creamy yogurt tzatziki accented with mint and cucumber,
and a smoky grilled eggplant dip puréed with fresh herbs and green onion. Serve together or
individually with pita triangles and crunchy vegetable sticks.*

CREAMY HUMMUS

1	can (19 oz/540 mL) chick-peas, drained and rinsed	1
1/2 cup	tahini	125 mL
1/3 cup	olive oil	75 mL
1/3 cup	lemon juice	75 mL
1/2 tsp	ground coriander	2 mL
1/4 tsp	ground cumin	1 mL
2	large cloves garlic, minced	2
3 tbsp	chopped fresh parsley	50 mL
	Salt and pepper	

● In food processor, purée chick-peas, tahini, oil, lemon juice, coriander and cumin until smooth; transfer to bowl.

● Stir in garlic, parsley and 1/4 cup (50 mL) water. Season with salt and pepper to taste. Makes 3 cups (750 mL).

TIPS
● Tahini, a paste made of ground sesame seeds, is available at specialty and health food stores.
● Be sure to stir the water into the dip *after* processing or it will simply be absorbed and not make the dip creamy.

GRILLED EGGPLANT DIP

2	eggplants (about 2 lb/1 kg)	2
2	cloves garlic, minced	2
1	green onion, minced	1
2 tbsp	chopped fresh parsley	25 mL
2 tbsp	olive oil	25 mL
1 tbsp	chopped fresh basil	15 mL
1 tbsp	lemon juice	15 mL
1 tsp	Dijon mustard	5 mL
	Salt and pepper	

● With fork, prick eggplants. Grill over medium-high heat, turning occasionally, for 45 to 50 minutes or until tender and charred all over. Let stand on plate until cool enough to handle, reserving juices.

● Cut eggplants in half lengthwise. With spoon, scoop flesh into food processor, adding any juices from plate; purée. Transfer to bowl.

● Stir in garlic, onion, parsley, oil, basil, lemon juice and mustard. Season with salt and pepper to taste. Makes 2 cups (500 mL).

MINTED TZATZIKI

2 cups	plain yogurt	500 mL
Half	English cucumber	Half
1/2 tsp	salt	2 mL
2 tbsp	chopped fresh mint	25 mL
1 tbsp	each olive oil and lemon juice	15 mL
3	cloves garlic, minced	3
1/4 tsp	pepper	1 mL

● Line sieve with double thickness of cheesecloth; set over bowl. Add yogurt and drain in refrigerator for at least 3 hours or up to 24 hours until reduced to about 1 cup (250 mL).

● Peel and grate cucumber into another sieve; sprinkle with half of the salt. Let drain for 1 hour.

● In bowl, stir together drained yogurt and cucumber, remaining salt, mint, oil, lemon juice, garlic and pepper. Makes 1-1/2 cups (375 mL).

TIP: You can drain the cucumber ahead of time, but don't stir it into the yogurt mixture until just ready to serve.

(clockwise from left) Grilled Eggplant Dip, Creamy Hummus and Minted Tzatziki

Grilled Peppers with Shaved Asiago

For an appetizer that is simplicity itself, drizzle grilled peppers with extra virgin olive oil, then top with whisper-thin shavings of Asiago cheese and freshly ground black pepper.

3	large sweet peppers	3
2 tbsp	extra virgin olive oil	25 mL
8	paper-thin slices Asiago cheese	8
	Pepper	

● Broil or grill sweet peppers, turning several times, for about 20 minutes or until blistered and charred. Peel, seed and cut lengthwise into quarters.

● Attractively arrange 3 pieces of sweet pepper on each plate; drizzle with oil. Top each with cheese; sprinkle with pepper to taste. Makes 4 servings.

Italian Potato Croquettes

Gooey with melting mozzarella in the middle and crisp on the outside, these potato croquettes are part of the selection of antipasti at Grano, a trendsetting bakery/café in Toronto.

3-1/2 lb	baking potatoes	1.7 kg
2	eggs, beaten	2
1/2 cup	freshly grated Parmesan cheese	125 mL
1/3 cup	minced fresh parsley	75 mL
3	large cloves garlic, minced	3
1/2 tsp	salt	2 mL
1/4 tsp	pepper	1 mL
8 oz	mozzarella cheese, cut into 3/4-inch (2 cm) cubes	250 g
1/3 cup	all-purpose flour	75 mL
	Vegetable oil for deep-frying	
	Escarole lettuce	
	Sweet red and green pepper strips	

● Scrub potatoes. In large pot of boiling salted water, cook potatoes for about 25 minutes or until tender. Drain and let cool enough to handle; peel and place in large bowl.

● With hands, squeeze potatoes to mash to almost smooth purée with a few pea-size pieces. Add eggs, Parmesan, parsley, garlic, salt and pepper, mixing with hands until mixture holds together.

● Divide into 24 portions. Press 1 mozzarella cube into middle of each portion; cover with potato mixture, forming oval about 2-1/2 inches (6 cm) long. Dust with flour, tapping off excess; place on floured baking sheet. Refrigerate for at least 30 minutes or until firm. Dust again with flour, tapping off excess.

● In deep-fryer or deep pot, heat oil to 375°F (190°C) on deep-fryer thermometer, or until 1-inch (2.5 cm) cube of white bread turns golden brown in 40 seconds. Deep-fry croquettes, a few at a time, for about 2 minutes or until golden brown.

● With slotted spoon, transfer to rack to drain. Serve hot if desired, or let cool, arrange on lettuce-lined platter and garnish with lattice of red and green peppers. Makes 24 croquettes.

POTATO HAND WARMERS

After the sleigh ride, when everyone's back from skating or in from playing outside, a basket of baked potatoes is a warming treat.

● Simply bake potatoes in 400°F (200°C) oven for 45 to 60 minutes, then slice almost in half lengthwise, sprinkle with salt and pepper to taste and insert a finger of tasty cheese such as Cheddar, Monterey Jack, Edam or Swiss. Close up, wrap in a napkin and serve in a basket.

Creamy Guacamole

3	ripe avocados	3
1/4 cup	finely chopped onion	50 mL
1	clove garlic, minced	1
1	jalapeño pepper, finely chopped	1
3 tbsp	lime or lemon juice	50 mL
2 tbsp	chopped fresh coriander	25 mL
1/2 tsp	salt	2 mL

● Peel and mash avocados. In bowl, combine avocados, onion, garlic, jalapeño pepper, lime juice, coriander and salt. *(Guacamole can be covered with plastic wrap directly on surface and refrigerated for up to 8 hours.)* Makes about 2-1/2 cups (625 mL).

Instead of scooping up guacamole with salty fried corn chips, cut flour tortillas into wedges, brush lightly with oil and crisp in a 350°F (180°C) oven for about 8 minutes or until golden.

TIP: If making guacamole ahead, the trick is to keep it from going brown. Try burying one of the avocado pits in it and covering the surface directly with plastic wrap.

Tomato Salsa with Peppered Cheese

2 cups	shredded Cheddar cheese	500 mL
1	pkg (250 g) cream cheese or creamy goat cheese (chèvre)	1
1 tbsp	Dijon mustard	15 mL
1/2 tsp	pepper	2 mL
1/2 tsp	hot pepper sauce	2 mL
1 cup	crushed corn chips	250 mL
	SALSA	
6	tomatoes	6
1/2 cup	each chopped fresh parsley and coriander	125 mL
4	green onions, chopped	4
2	jalapeño peppers, finely chopped	2
2	cloves garlic, minced	2
1/2 tsp	salt	2 mL

● Press rounds into corn chips to coat well on both sides. Bake on greased baking sheet in 400°F (200°C) oven for 3 to 5 minutes or until cheese is spreadable but not runny.

● Meanwhile, with slotted spoon, arrange salsa on plates; top with cheese rounds. Makes 8 servings.

TIPS

● If coriander isn't available, use more fresh parsley and 1/2 tsp (2 mL) grated lemon rind.
● When handling hot jalapeño peppers, wear plastic or rubber gloves.

While "quick" is important in these busy times, make-ahead is another excellent way to cut back on last-minute fussing when entertaining. This appetizer takes a little time to make, but both the cheese rounds and the salsa are make-ahead — a combo everyone will enjoy, including the cook.

● SALSA: Core, seed and finely dice tomatoes; drain well in sieve. In bowl, combine tomatoes, parsley, coriander, onions, jalapeño peppers, garlic and salt. *(Salsa can be covered and refrigerated for up to 24 hours; drain well.)*

● In bowl, beat together Cheddar, cream cheese, mustard, pepper and hot pepper sauce. Shape into eight 1/2-inch (1 cm) thick rounds. *(Rounds can be covered and refrigerated for up to 24 hours.)*

NEW VEGGIES FOR DIPPING

There's more to a plate of crudités than carrot and celery sticks.
● Cut peeled rutabaga, the more exotic jicama and peeled broccoli stalks into sticks, too. Add florets from broccoli, cauliflower and the new-fangled green cauliflower/broccoli hybrid and spikey broccoflower (romanesco).
● Button mushrooms and cherry tomatoes make great little dippers and so do endive spears, tiny radicchio cups and sweet pepper strips.
● Or, try halved brussels sprouts, snap and snow peas, blanched green beans and asparagus, radishes and diagonally sliced golden and green zucchini.

Spinach and Cheese Phyllo Triangles ▶

Packets of paper-thin flaky pastry wrap up a crowd-pleasing filling of ricotta, Parmesan and spinach. These hors d'oeuvres triangles are freezable and ready to bake at a moment's notice — a definite plus for today's busy cooks.

10	sheets phyllo pastry	10
1/2 cup	butter, melted	125 mL
	SPINACH CHEESE FILLING	
1	pkg (10 oz/284 g) fresh spinach, trimmed	1
1 tbsp	olive oil	15 mL
2 tbsp	minced onion	25 mL
2	cloves garlic, minced	2
1 cup	ricotta cheese	250 mL
1/3 cup	freshly grated Parmesan cheese	75 mL
1/2 tsp	grated lemon rind	2 mL
Pinch	each salt, pepper and ground nutmeg	Pinch

● SPINACH CHEESE FILLING: Rinse spinach; shake off excess water. In large pot, cover spinach and cook over medium heat, with just the water clinging to leaves, for about 2 minutes or just until wilted. Drain well and squeeze dry; chop coarsely to make about 3/4 cup (175 mL).

● In skillet, heat oil over medium-high heat; cook onion and garlic, stirring occasionally, for 2 minutes or until softened.

● In bowl, stir together onion mixture, spinach, ricotta, Parmesan, lemon rind, salt, pepper and nutmeg; set aside.

● Place 1 sheet of the phyllo on work surface, keeping remaining phyllo covered with damp cloth to prevent drying out. Cut sheet lengthwise into 5 strips, each about 2-1/2 inches (6 cm) wide; brush strips with butter.

● Spoon heaping teaspoonful (5 mL) of the filling about 1/2 inch (1 cm) from end of each strip. Fold 1 corner of phyllo over filling so bottom edge meets side edge to form triangle. Fold up triangle.

● Continue folding triangle sideways and upward (like folding a flag) until end of phyllo strip. Fold end flap over to adhere. Working quickly, form triangles with remaining strips. Repeat with remaining phyllo sheets and filling.

● Place triangles on baking sheets; brush lightly with butter. *(Triangles can be prepared to this point and frozen on baking sheets. Store in airtight containers for up to 2 months. Do not thaw before baking.)* Bake in 375°F (190°C) oven for 15 to 18 minutes or until golden. Serve hot. Makes 50 appetizers.

TIP: A 1-lb (454 g) package of frozen phyllo pastry usually contains 20 sheets. To thaw, place the package in the refrigerator for about 24 hours. It's best to refreeze any remaining phyllo only once.

Roasted Tomatoes

Roasting, like drying, intensifies the flavor of vegetables. Tomatoes roast up delectably and make an impressive appetizer with toasted crusty bread and creamy goat cheese.

4	large tomatoes	4
2	cloves garlic	2
4 tsp	olive oil	20 mL
	Salt and pepper	

● Core tomatoes and cut in half crosswise; place, cut side up, in shallow baking dish. Quarter garlic lengthwise; press sliver into center of each tomato. Bake in 325°F (160°C) oven for 2 hours.

● Drizzle with oil and season with salt and pepper to taste; bake for 1 hour or until skins are wrinkled and cut surfaces look dried. Serve hot or at room temperature. Makes 4 servings.

Fiesta Cheesecake ◄

1 cup	ground blue tortilla chips	250 mL
3 tbsp	all-purpose flour	50 mL
2 tbsp	butter, melted	25 mL
2	pkg (each 250 g) cream cheese	2
3	eggs	3
1 tbsp	lime juice	15 mL
2 tsp	chili powder	10 mL
1-1/2 tsp	ground cumin	7 mL
1 tsp	dried oregano	5 mL
1/4 tsp	salt	1 mL
1/4 tsp	hot pepper sauce	1 mL
2 cups	sour cream	500 mL
	SALSA	
2 cups	chopped tomatoes	500 mL
1	each small sweet yellow and green pepper, diced	1
4	green onions, sliced	4
2	cloves garlic, minced	2
2 tbsp	chopped fresh coriander or parsley	25 mL
2 tbsp	lime juice	25 mL
1/4 tsp	hot pepper sauce	1 mL
	Salt and pepper	
	Tortilla chips	

● Combine ground tortilla chips, flour and butter; pat into bottom of greased 9-inch (2.5 L) springform pan. Center pan on large foil square; press up tightly to side of pan. Bake in 350°F (180°C) oven for 10 minutes. Remove from oven and set aside. Reduce oven temperature to 325°F (160°C).

● In large bowl, beat cream cheese until softened; beat in eggs, one at a time, beating well after each addition. Beat in lime juice, chili powder, cumin, oregano, salt and hot pepper sauce; blend in sour cream. Pour onto base.

● Set pan in larger pan; pour in enough hot water to come 1 inch (2.5 cm) up side. Bake for about 35 minutes or until edge is set but center still jiggles slightly. Quickly run knife around inside of pan. Turn oven off; let cool in oven for 1 hour.

● Remove pan from larger pan and remove foil; let cool on rack to room temperature. Cover and refrigerate for at least 8 hours or until chilled. *(Cheesecake can be refrigerated for up to 2 days.)* Let stand at room temperature for 30 minutes. Transfer to serving platter.

● SALSA: In bowl, combine tomatoes, peppers, onions, garlic, coriander, lime juice, hot pepper sauce, and salt and pepper to taste. Using slotted spoon, spoon over cheesecake. Serve with tortilla chips. Makes 20 servings.

TIP: For 1 cup (250 mL) ground tortilla chips, use about two-thirds of a 7-oz (198 g) bag of tortilla chips — blue, if available, for color contrast with the filling.

Fresh salsa, tortilla chips and a zippy cheesecake bring the sunny flavors of Mexico to your table. Easy to make, this crowd-pleaser keeps for up to 2 days in the refrigerator.

Seasonal Salads

Salad days are not just summer days. Every season offers a salad to enjoy — from tender shoots and sprouts in the spring to the robust tomatoes of summer, autumnal cabbages and winter's grated carrots.

Summertime Potato Salad ▶

When the sun shines, forget about mashing or frying potatoes — it's definitely potato salad time! There's no tastier partner to easy cold meat or fish plate suppers. And even if you have a favorite potato salad recipe, why not try our delicious take on a summer classic.

10	new potatoes (about 2-1/2 lb/1.25 kg)	10
10	large radishes, thinly sliced	10
2	stalks celery, finely diced	2
6	green onions, chopped	6
	DRESSING	
1/4 cup	white wine vinegar	50 mL
2 tsp	Dijon mustard	10 mL
1	clove garlic, minced	1
1/2 tsp	salt	2 mL
1/4 tsp	pepper	1 mL
1/3 cup	vegetable oil	75 mL
2 tbsp	chopped fresh parsley	25 mL

● Scrub potatoes; cut in half if large. In saucepan, cover potatoes with cold water and bring to boil; cook for 10 to 15 minutes or just until tender but not mushy. Drain and return to pot to dry over low heat for 30 seconds. Arrange in single layer on towel-lined work surface; let cool.

● Peel potatoes and cut into 3/4-inch (2 cm) cubes; place in large bowl. Add radishes, celery and onions.

● DRESSING: In small bowl, whisk together vinegar, mustard, garlic, salt and pepper; gradually whisk in oil. Stir in parsley. Pour over potato mixture; gently toss to coat well. Makes 4 to 6 servings.

TIP: Buy potatoes of the same size so that they will cook evenly. Boiling potatoes with skins on helps to keep them intact while cooking.

Broccoli Slaw

Two nutrient-rich vegetables team up in a colorful salad that's delicious any season of the year.

1	bunch broccoli	1
1	large carrot, grated	1
1/3 cup	sliced green onions	75 mL
1/3 cup	slivered radishes	75 mL
	DRESSING	
2 tbsp	red wine vinegar	25 mL
1	clove garlic, minced	1
1 tsp	Dijon mustard	5 mL
Pinch	each salt and pepper	Pinch
3 tbsp	vegetable oil	50 mL

● Cut florets from broccoli stems; reserve florets for another use. Peel and grate stems. In large bowl, toss together grated broccoli, carrot, onions and radishes.

● DRESSING: In small bowl, whisk together vinegar, garlic, mustard, salt and pepper; gradually whisk in oil. Toss with broccoli mixture. Makes 4 servings.

Potato Salad Roll

Our recent Heritage Recipe Contest welcomed readers' recipes from across Canada. Pamela Beedle of London, Ontario, contributed this novel potato salad that the judging team of Rose Murray, Carol Ferguson and Marg Fraser chose for taste and presentation.

3 cups	cold mashed potatoes (about 7 potatoes)	750 mL
1/3 cup	mayonnaise	75 mL
2 tsp	chopped onion	10 mL
2 tsp	milk	10 mL
1/2 tsp	salt	2 mL
1/2 tsp	paprika	2 mL
3 tbsp	chopped fresh parsley	50 mL
	Lettuce leaves	
	FILLING	
6	hard-cooked eggs, chopped	6
1/4 cup	each finely chopped sweet green pepper and pimientos	50 mL
2 tbsp	mayonnaise	25 mL
1/4 tsp	salt	1 mL
Pinch	pepper	Pinch

● FILLING: In bowl, stir together eggs, green pepper, pimientos, mayonnaise, salt and pepper; set aside.

● In separate bowl, stir together potatoes, mayonnaise, onion, milk, salt and paprika. Evenly spread on large sheet of waxed paper into 12- x 8-inch (30 x 20 cm) rectangle.

● Spread filling over top; roll up, jelly roll-style, using waxed paper to aid rolling. Sprinkle with parsley. Cover and refrigerate for at least 2 hours or until chilled. *(Roll can be refrigerated for up to 1 day.)* Slice and serve on lettuce leaves. Makes 12 servings.

Orange Sesame Asparagus and Greens

In a well-dressed salad, the vinaigrette complements the greens without overwhelming them. Orange and sesame flavors do just that for an inventive toss of endive, radicchio, watercress and spring asparagus. In summer, replace the asparagus with green beans.

8 oz	asparagus, trimmed	250 g
1 tbsp	sesame seeds	15 mL
Half	head curly endive	Half
Half	head radicchio or red leaf lettuce	Half
1	bunch watercress	1
1	Belgian endive	1
	ORANGE SESAME DRESSING	
2 tsp	grated orange rind	10 mL
1/4 cup	orange juice	50 mL
2 tbsp	finely chopped fresh basil (or 2 tsp/10 mL dried)	25 mL
2 tbsp	white wine vinegar	25 mL
2 tsp	Dijon mustard	10 mL
1 tsp	sesame oil (optional)	5 mL
1/4 tsp	each salt and pepper	1 mL
1/4 cup	vegetable oil	50 mL

● In pot of boiling salted water, blanch asparagus for 2 to 3 minutes or until tender-crisp; refresh under cold water and drain well.

● In small skillet, toast sesame seeds over medium heat, shaking pan, for about 2 minutes or until golden; set aside.

● ORANGE SESAME DRESSING: In small bowl, combine orange rind and juice, basil, vinegar, mustard, sesame oil (if using), salt and pepper; gradually whisk in vegetable oil.

● Trim and separate leaves of curly endive, radicchio, watercress and Belgian endive; place in bowl. Toss with 1/2 cup (125 mL) of the dressing to lightly coat; arrange on large serving platter. Top with blanched asparagus; drizzle with remaining dressing. Sprinkle with sesame seeds. Makes 4 servings.

Grilled Vegetable Salad ▲

1	eggplant	1
2	large zucchini	2
1	each sweet red, green and yellow pepper	1
2 tbsp	olive oil	25 mL
2 tbsp	balsamic vinegar	25 mL
2 tbsp	chopped fresh thyme (or 1/4 tsp/1 mL dried)	25 mL
1 tbsp	water	15 mL
	Salt and pepper	

● Cut eggplant into 1/2-inch (1 cm) thick slices; arrange in steamer in single layer. Steam for 4 minutes.

● Cut zucchini diagonally into 1/4-inch (5 mm) thick slices. Seed and cut peppers lengthwise into 8 pieces. Brush zucchini lightly with 1 tsp (5 mL) of the oil.

● Grill eggplant, zucchini and peppers, in batches if necessary, over high heat for 4 to 6 minutes on each side or until tender but firm. Transfer to serving bowl.

● Whisk together remaining oil, vinegar, thyme, water, and salt and pepper to taste; toss with hot vegetables. Makes 6 servings.

TIP: Steaming the eggplant before grilling keeps it moist and shortens the grilling time.

T*he darling of the restaurant scene, grilled vegetables dressed and presented with panache translate perfectly to the home kitchen and barbecue. Since grilled vegetables keep well for up to a day, this spunky salad is ideal for picnics or other weekend occasions.*

Salade Composée ▼

A feature of French bistros, this array of vegetables arranged beautifully on a plate and drizzled with a lightened-up dressing makes a wonderful lunch. Other ingredients can be added to the plate, depending on the contents of your refrigerator. They include grated celery root (celeriac), cold meats or flaked cooked fish.

4	beets	4
8	small new red potatoes	8
2/3 cup	Mustard Garlic Vinaigrette (recipe follows)	150 mL
	Lettuce leaves	
1-1/2 cups	grated carrots	375 mL
1 cup	cooked or canned corn kernels	250 mL
1	can (19 oz/540 mL) chick-peas, drained and rinsed	1
1/4 cup	chopped fresh parsley	50 mL
1 tsp	ground cumin	5 mL
4	slices smoked turkey, rolled	4

● Scrub beets; trim stems 1 inch (2.5 cm) from bulb. In pot of boiling water, cook beets for about 40 minutes or until tender. Drain and refresh under cold water; slip off skins. Slice beets and set aside.

● In pot of boiling water, cook potatoes for 20 minutes or until tender. Drain and return to pot; shake over medium heat until dry. Cut in half and set aside.

● Toss beets with 2 tbsp (25 mL) of the Mustard Garlic Vinaigrette; divide among lettuce-lined plates. Repeat with potatoes, carrots, then corn. Combine chick-peas, parsley and cumin; toss with 2 tbsp (25 mL) of the vinaigrette and divide among plates. Top with turkey. Makes 4 servings.

MUSTARD GARLIC VINAIGRETTE

1/3 cup	water	75 mL
2 tbsp	white wine vinegar	25 mL
1 tbsp	Dijon mustard	15 mL
1/2 tsp	granulated sugar	2 mL
1	clove garlic, minced	1
1/3 cup	vegetable oil	75 mL
2 tsp	freshly grated Parmesan cheese	10 mL
	Salt and pepper	

● In small bowl, whisk together water, vinegar, mustard, sugar and garlic; gradually whisk in oil. Stir in Parmesan. Season with salt and pepper to taste. Makes 1 cup (250 mL).

Bodybuilder Broccoli Salad

3 cups	broccoli florets (1 bunch)	750 mL
1/2 cup	sliced red onion	125 mL
1/2 cup	sunflower seeds	125 mL
1/2 cup	raisins	125 mL
1/2 cup	crumbled feta cheese	125 mL
	DRESSING	
1/2 cup	plain yogurt	125 mL
1/4 cup	mayonnaise	50 mL
2 tbsp	granulated sugar	25 mL
1 tbsp	lemon juice	15 mL
	Salt and pepper	

● In bowl, combine broccoli, onion, sunflower seeds, raisins and feta cheese.

● DRESSING: Stir together yogurt, mayonnaise, sugar and lemon juice; toss with salad. Season with salt and pepper to taste. Cover and refrigerate for 2 hours. *(Salad can be refrigerated for up to 1 day.)* Makes 6 servings.

A *powerhouse of nutrients, broccoli contains calcium, iron and vitamin C to aid iron absorption. Feta cheese and yogurt add extra calcium and a tasty creaminess to the salad.*

Spinach Sensation

1	pkg (10 oz/284 g) fresh spinach	1
2	hard-cooked eggs, chopped	2
1 cup	croutons	250 mL
1/2 cup	sliced mushrooms	125 mL
4	strips bacon, cooked and crumbled	4
	DRESSING	
1/4 cup	chopped Spanish onion	50 mL
1/4 cup	fresh parsley sprigs	50 mL
1 tbsp	diced pimiento	15 mL
2	cloves garlic	2
1/4 cup	mayonnaise	50 mL
2 tbsp	ketchup	25 mL
1 tbsp	lemon juice	15 mL
1 tbsp	red wine vinegar	15 mL
2 tsp	anchovy paste	10 mL
1/4 tsp	each salt and pepper	1 mL

● Trim and tear spinach into bite-size pieces; place in salad bowl. Add eggs, croutons, mushrooms and bacon.

● DRESSING: In food processor or blender, purée onion, parsley and pimiento; with machine running, drop garlic through feed tube. Add mayonnaise, ketchup, lemon juice, vinegar, anchovy paste, salt and pepper; purée until blended. Toss with salad. Makes 8 servings.

S*pinach salad is one of those culinary canvases that inspires chefs to be creative. Here's the chock-full-of-goodies rendition from Thackeray's in Halifax, and it's mighty good — as the line-up crowds at this restaurant will attest.*

STEMS OR STEMLESS?
When cooking spinach, just trim the ends off spinach stems. For raw in salads, trim off long stems near leaf, leaving shorter and crisp tender stems on smaller inner leaves.

Curried Corn and Chicken Salad

This salad is lovely served on a radicchio or red lettuce leaf, or spooned into a juicy red tomato that's been quartered almost to the base and separated to hold the salad.

3 cups	cooked or canned corn kernels	750 mL
2 cups	cubed cooked chicken	500 mL
1 cup	shredded red cabbage (or coarsely chopped tomato)	250 mL
1	sweet green pepper, chopped	1
1	carrot, diced	1
1/3 cup	chopped red onion	75 mL
	DRESSING	
1/2 cup	plain yogurt	125 mL
1/4 cup	mayonnaise	50 mL
1 tsp	each curry powder and packed brown sugar	5 mL
1 tsp	cider vinegar	5 mL
1/2 tsp	each ground cumin, salt and pepper	2 mL

● In large bowl, combine corn, chicken, cabbage, green pepper, carrot and onion.

● DRESSING: Whisk together yogurt, mayonnaise, curry powder, sugar, vinegar, cumin, salt and pepper; toss with salad. *(Salad can be covered and refrigerated for up to 4 hours.)* Makes 4 servings.

Light Vegetable Pasta Salad

When pasta salads are made ahead, the pasta tends to absorb the dressing and make the salad dry. To provide that needed moisture at serving time, add about 1/4 cup (50 mL) milk instead of more oil. The result will be just as tasty, and much lighter.

1 cup	broccoli florets	250 mL
4 cups	cooked pasta	1 L
1 cup	shredded carrots	250 mL
1/2 cup	sliced mushrooms	125 mL
1/2 cup	diced cooked ham	125 mL
1/4 cup	chopped green onions	50 mL
2 tbsp	chopped fresh dill or parsley	25 mL
1 cup	plain yogurt	250 mL
1/2 cup	light mayonnaise	125 mL
2 tbsp	white wine vinegar	25 mL
2 tbsp	Dijon mustard	25 mL
	Salt and pepper	

● In pot of boiling water, cook broccoli for about 1 minute or until bright green; drain and refresh under cold water. Drain and pat dry; place in bowl. Add pasta, carrots, mushrooms, ham, onions and dill.

● Whisk together yogurt, mayonnaise, vinegar and mustard; toss half with salad. Refrigerate for 1 hour. Fold in remaining dressing. *(Salad can be covered and refrigerated for up to 1 day.)* Season with salt and pepper to taste. Makes 8 servings.

Tomato Salad Provençale

This is salad at its easiest and most full-flavored — just ripe and juicy tomatoes with olive oil, lemon juice, garlic and an authentic garnish of oil-cured black olives.

2	large tomatoes	2
1/4 cup	finely chopped black olives	50 mL
1/4 cup	finely diced celery	50 mL
4 tsp	chopped fresh parsley	20 mL
2 tbsp	olive oil	25 mL
2 tsp	lemon juice	10 mL
1	clove garlic, minced	1
	Salt and pepper	
	Thin strips lemon rind	

● Cut tomatoes in half crosswise; scoop out seeds from each half. Place tomatoes, cut side up, in serving dish. Sprinkle with olives, celery and parsley.

● Whisk together oil, lemon juice, garlic, and salt and pepper to taste; spoon over tomatoes. Garnish with lemon rind. Makes 4 servings.

(clockwise from top) Red Barn Corn and Bean Salad, Roasted Red Pepper Mayo (p. 89),
Creamy Guacamole (p. 65) and Quick 'n' Easy Pickle Slices (p. 87)

Red Barn Corn and Bean Salad ▲

1	can (19 oz/540 mL) chick-peas, drained and rinsed	1
1	can (19 oz/540 mL) red kidney beans, drained and rinsed	1
1	can (15 oz/425 g) black beans, drained and rinsed	1
1	can (12 oz/341 mL) corn kernels, drained	1
1/2 cup	chopped red onion	125 mL
1	sweet red pepper, diced	1
1/2 cup	chopped celery	125 mL
	DRESSING	
1/2 cup	chopped fresh basil (or 1 tbsp/15 mL dried)	125 mL
1/2 cup	red wine vinegar	125 mL

1/3 cup	olive oil	75 mL
1 tbsp	Dijon mustard	15 mL
1	clove garlic, minced	1
1-1/2 tsp	salt	7 mL
1/2 tsp	hot pepper sauce	2 mL
1/2 tsp	pepper	2 mL
1/4 cup	chopped fresh parsley	50 mL

● In large bowl, combine chick-peas, kidney beans, black beans, corn, onion, red pepper and celery; set aside.

● DRESSING: Whisk together basil, vinegar, oil, mustard, garlic, salt, hot pepper sauce and pepper; toss with bean mixture. *(Salad can be covered and refrigerated for up to 1 day.)* Garnish with parsley. Makes 12 servings.

For the last few summers, Canadian Living's Food Department has assisted CBC Radio's "Morningside" program host, Peter Gzowski, and Shelley Ambrose at The Red Barn Show and Barbecue — the kick-off event to the Peter Gzowski Invitational, an annual golf tournament and fund-raiser for literacy. This updated quick and easy bean salad is one of the delicious crowd-pleasers.

Green Bean Salad with Julienne of Turkey ▲

Leftover turkey or chicken is worth its weight in gold and convenience. Serve these light salad plates with whole-grain rolls and finish with fruit-topped yogurt for dessert.

2 tbsp	cider vinegar	25 mL
1 tbsp	olive oil	15 mL
1	clove garlic, minced	1
1 tsp	Dijon mustard	5 mL
1/2 tsp	salt	2 mL
1/4 tsp	granulated sugar	1 mL
1/4 tsp	cracked peppercorns	1 mL
1/2 cup	slivered red onion	125 mL
1 lb	green beans	500 g
1	bay leaf	1
8 oz	cooked turkey, sliced	250 g
1 cup	cherry tomatoes, quartered	250 mL
	Red lettuce leaves	
2 tbsp	chopped fresh parsley	25 mL

● In large bowl, whisk together vinegar, oil, garlic, mustard, salt, sugar and peppercorns; add onion and toss well. Set aside.

● In large pot of boiling salted water, cook beans and bay leaf for 5 to 7 minutes or until beans are tender-crisp. Drain and refresh under cold water, discarding bay leaf; drain again and pat dry. Add to bowl.

● Cut turkey into strips; add to bowl along with tomatoes. Toss to coat well. Serve on lettuce-lined plates; garnish with parsley. Makes 4 servings.

Fairouz Salad

6	radishes, quartered	6
3	tomatoes, cubed	3
1	cucumber, peeled, seeded and cubed	1
1	sweet green pepper, coarsely chopped	1
1	small mild white or Spanish onion, coarsely chopped	1
1	head romaine lettuce, chopped	1
1	whole wheat pita bread	1
1 cup	chopped fresh parsley	250 mL
1 tbsp	chopped fresh mint	15 mL
	DRESSING	
1/3 cup	lemon juice	75 mL
1/3 cup	olive oil	75 mL
2 tsp	sumac spice (optional)	10 mL
3/4 tsp	salt	4 mL

● In large bowl, combine radishes, tomatoes, cucumber, green pepper, onion and lettuce.

● Separate pita bread into rounds; broil, turning once, for 2 minutes or until crisp. Break into 1/2-inch (1 cm) pieces.

● DRESSING: Whisk together lemon juice, oil, sumac spice (if using) and salt; pour over vegetables. Add parsley, mint and pita pieces; toss lightly to coat. Makes 6 to 8 servings.

TIP: Sumac spice is a typical Middle Eastern flavoring and it's available in many cities across the country where there is a Lebanese community.

From the excellent Ottawa restaurant, Fairouz, comes a delicious example of healthful Lebanese cuisine with its emphasis on salads, vegetables and grains.

Grilled Pepper and Fennel Salad

2	each sweet red and yellow peppers	2
2	fennel bulbs	2
3 tbsp	olive oil	50 mL
1/2 cup	pitted black olives	125 mL
2 tbsp	chopped fresh basil	25 mL
1	head romaine lettuce	1
	DRESSING	
3 tbsp	balsamic vinegar	50 mL
1/2 tsp	salt	2 mL
1/2 tsp	pepper	2 mL
1	clove garlic, minced	1
1/3 cup	olive oil	75 mL

● Grill red and yellow peppers, turning several times, for about 20 minutes or until blistered and charred. Let cool; peel, seed and cut into bite-size chunks, reserving juices. Place peppers in bowl; set aside.

● Meanwhile, trim top and bottom of fennel. Separate layers; slice lengthwise. Brush lightly with some of the oil; grill, turning once and brushing with oil, for 10 to 12 minutes or until tender-crisp. Cut into bite-size chunks; add to peppers. Add olives and basil.

● DRESSING: In small bowl, combine vinegar, salt, pepper, garlic and reserved juice from peppers; gradually whisk in oil. Toss with pepper mixture. *(Salad can be refrigerated for up to 24 hours.)* Serve in lettuce-lined bowl. Makes 8 appetizer or 4 main-course servings.

An ideal appetizer salad has more going for it than a few leaves of lettuce and wedges of tomato. Cooking school owner and food writer Bonnie Stern leads the way with this inventive union of grilled peppers and fennel. Greek or Italian olives are best; avoid the bland canned ones.

Preserves and Sauces

Add flavor and crunch to any meal with summer's store of pickles and relishes — or splash on the fresh tastes of the garden with easy vinaigrettes, sauces and salsas.

Spicy Pearl Onion Sours ▶

Two unusual spices — green peppercorns and juniper berries — join cinnamon and cloves to flavor tiny pearl onions. This fine preserve deserves to be tucked away for sharing only with your favorite people!

TIP: Look for green peppercorns and juniper berries in specialty stores, or in well-stocked spice sections of the supermarket.

2 lb	pearl onions	1 kg
1/4 cup	pickling salt	50 mL
3 cups	white vinegar	750 mL
2 tbsp	granulated sugar	25 mL
1 tbsp	juniper berries	15 mL
1	stick cinnamon	1
2 tsp	whole cloves	10 mL
2 tsp	green peppercorns	10 mL
3	sprigs fresh tarragon	3

● In heatproof bowl, cover onions with boiling water; let stand for 1 minute. Drain and peel.

● In bowl, cover onions and salt with cold water; let stand for 8 hours or overnight. Drain and rinse well in cold water; drain well.

● In large heavy saucepan, combine vinegar, sugar, juniper berries, cinnamon, cloves and peppercorns; bring to boil. Remove from heat; cover and let stand for at least 30 minutes or up to 2 hours. Strain out spices and discard, reserving vinegar mixture in saucepan. Return to boil.

● Place tarragon sprig in each of three 2-cup (500 mL) hot sterilized canning jars. Pack onions into jars; pour vinegar mixture over top, leaving 1/2-inch (1.25 cm) headspace. Seal and process in boiling water bath for 10 minutes (see Preserving Basics, p. 83). Makes about 6 cups (1.5 L).

CLOSE-UP ON ONIONS

Choose Well
● Choose firm dry-skinned onions with no signs of sprouting.

Quantity
● Four average onions total about 1 lb (500 g). Each onion produces about 1 cup (250 mL) chopped.

● Pearl or pickling onions are often sold in 2-cup (500 mL) plastic containers, or by weight.

Storage
● Store onions away from potatoes in cool, dark, well-ventilated spot.

● Spanish onions, with their higher sugar content, do not keep as well as the common yellow onion.

Preparation
● Trim off stem and root ends; lift off strip of skin from top down to root end. Pull dry outer skin off moister inner layers.

● For pearl onions, cover with boiling water and let stand for 30 to 60 seconds. Trim ends and pull off thin outer layer. Cut shallow X in root end to prevent onions from breaking apart during cooking.

Cooking Basics
● Bake, braise or sauté onions. Boil or steam small onions only.

Nutrition Note
● Contribute vitamin C, folate and fiber.

(on window sill and to left) Spicy Pearl Onion Sours; (in jar with spoon) Taco Sauce (p.82)

Green Tomato Hotdog Relish

Often called end-of-garden relish because it uses up the last of the vegetable harvest, this mustardy condiment is also tasty with ham and all cold meats. Or, for a colorful twist, stir a little into cabbage salad.

12	green tomatoes	12
3	cucumbers, peeled and seeded	3
6	onions	6
6	sweet red peppers, seeded	6
1/3 cup	pickling salt	75 mL
4 cups	granulated sugar	1 L
3-1/4 cups	cider vinegar	800 mL
1 tsp	celery seeds	5 mL
1 tsp	mustard seeds	5 mL
2 tbsp	all-purpose flour	25 mL
2 tsp	dry mustard	10 mL
1 tsp	turmeric	5 mL

● In food processor or by hand, coarsely chop tomatoes, cucumbers, onions and red peppers.

● In large nonaluminum bowl, sprinkle vegetables with salt; mix well and let stand in cool place overnight. Drain and rinse under cold water; drain again.

● In large nonaluminum saucepan, combine sugar, 3 cups (750 mL) of the vinegar, celery seeds and mustard seeds; bring to boil. Stir in vegetables and return to boil; reduce heat and simmer, stirring occasionally, for 10 minutes.

● Combine remaining vinegar, flour, mustard and turmeric to form smooth paste; stir in a few spoonfuls of hot relish. Stir back into relish; cook, stirring, for at least 3 minutes or until thickened.

● Ladle into hot sterilized canning jars, leaving 1/2-inch (1.25 cm) headspace. Seal and process in boiling water bath for 10 minutes (see Preserving Basics, next page). Makes about 12 cups (3 L).

Taco Sauce

Get a head start on fast taco fixings with this smartly seasoned sauce, then keep it handy for snack attacks and casual meals. (Photo, p. 81)

16 cups	coarsely chopped tomatoes (about 8-3/4 lb/4 kg)	4 L
1 cup	chopped onions	250 mL
1 cup	cider vinegar	250 mL
2	cloves garlic, minced	2
1/2 cup	granulated sugar	125 mL
2 tbsp	chili powder	25 mL
1 tsp	salt	5 mL
1 tsp	ground cumin	5 mL
1/2 tsp	cayenne pepper	2 mL

● In large saucepan, combine tomatoes, onions, vinegar and garlic; bring to boil. Reduce heat; cover and simmer for about 1 hour or until very tender.

● Press through food mill or sieve into clean saucepan. Stir in sugar, chili powder, salt, cumin and cayenne pepper; bring to boil. Reduce heat and simmer, stirring often, for about 25 minutes or until thick enough to coat spoon.

● Ladle into hot sterilized canning jars, leaving 1/2-inch (1.25 cm) headspace. Seal and process in boiling water bath for 30 minutes (see Preserving Basics, next page). Makes about 8 cups (2 L).

PRESERVING BASICS

Equipment

● The right equipment will make preserving a lot easier and safer. Tongs, heatproof measuring cups, wide-mouthed funnels, jar lifter, clean dishcloths, large heavy-bottomed saucepan or Dutch oven, large boiling water bath canner and canning jars with two-piece lids are enough to start with.

● Use only perfect canning jars free from nicks or scratches, and rust-free and unbent screw bands.

● Always use new discs to ensure a good and safe seal.

Preparation

● Wash jars and bands in hot sudsy water; rinse and let dry.

● Fill boiling water bath canner about two-thirds full of water. About 30 minutes before filling jars, bring to boil. Boil a kettle of water and keep handy to add to canner after adding jars.

● For filled jars that will be processed in boiling water bath for less than 10 minutes, extra sterilization is required. Place jars, 1/2-cup (125 mL) measure for pouring, kitchen knife and metal funnel in canner rack; lower into boiling water bath and boil for 15 minutes before filling. Remove jars from canner with tongs and fill immediately.

● Set a small pot of water on stove, ready to boil discs for 5 minutes before filling jars.

Filling Jars

● Fill jars, using prepared funnel and measure to avoid slopping preserve onto rims of jars. Always leave recommended headspace, generally 1/4 inch (5 mm) for jams, jellies, marmalades and conserves, 1/2 inch (1.25 cm) for pickles, relishes and chutneys.

● Using sterilized knife, press out any air bubbles; add more preserve if necessary to re-establish headspace. Center prepared disc on jar and apply screw band until fingertip tight.

Processing

● Place jars in rack set on edge of canner; lower into hot water and pour in enough of the extra heated water to cover jars by 2 inches (5 cm). Cover with lid; bring to boil and time processing once water boils.

● Using jar lifter, transfer jars from canner to rack or folded towel. Check for seal: if the disc snaps down, curving downward, satisfactory seal has occurred.

● Any improperly sealed jars should be refrigerated and used as soon as possible (within 3 weeks, for pickles and relishes).

Storing

● All preserves, jams, jellies, pickles and relishes should be kept in a cool, dark and dry place. Once a jar is opened, store it in the refrigerator.

Prizewinning Chili Sauce

12 cups	chopped peeled tomatoes (about 7 lb/3.15 kg)	3 L
2	large onions, chopped	2
2	sweet red peppers, chopped	2
2-3/4 cups	white vinegar	675 mL
1 cup	granulated sugar	250 mL
1 tsp	each ground ginger and nutmeg	5 mL
1 tsp	salt	5 mL
1/2 tsp	ground cloves	2 mL

● In large Dutch oven, combine tomatoes, onions, red peppers, vinegar, sugar, ginger, nutmeg, salt and cloves; bring to boil. Reduce heat and simmer, stirring often, for 1 hour.

● Transfer about one-quarter of the mixture to food processor or blender; purée until smooth. Return to pan and simmer for 15 to 20 minutes longer or until thickened.

● Ladle into hot sterilized canning jars, leaving 1/2-inch (1.25 cm) headspace. Seal and process in boiling water bath for 15 minutes (see Preserving Basics, above). Makes about 9 cups (2.25 L).

This heritage recipe from Miriam Fawcett of Hamilton, Ontario, has garnered many a red ribbon at fall fairs.

Ruby Beet Chutney

Beets are a different take on the apples, pears and tomatoes that usually go into a chutney but their natural sweetness is a delight in this jewel-colored condiment.

8	large beets	8
1	lemon	1
3 cups	chopped peeled apples	750 mL
2 cups	chopped onions	500 mL
2 cups	granulated sugar	500 mL
2 cups	cider vinegar	500 mL
1/2 cup	raisins	125 mL
1/4 cup	diced candied ginger	50 mL
1 tsp	mustard seeds	5 mL
1/2 tsp	salt	2 mL
1/2 tsp	pepper	2 mL

● Trim beets, leaving tails intact and about 1 inch (2.5 cm) of the stems. In large pot of boiling water, cook beets for about 30 minutes or until tender. Drain and let cool; slip off skins and dice to make 4-1/2 cups (1.125 L).

● Meanwhile, with zester, remove rind from lemon. (Or, pare off thin outer rind and cut into thin strips.) Squeeze and strain juice into large heavy nonaluminum saucepan or Dutch oven.

● Stir in lemon rind, apples, onions, sugar, vinegar, raisins, ginger, mustard seeds, salt and pepper; bring to boil. Reduce heat to low; simmer, stirring occasionally, for 30 minutes or until apples are tender. Stir in beets. Cook for 10 to 15 minutes or until thickened.

● Ladle into hot sterilized canning jars, leaving 1/2-inch (1.25 cm) headspace. Seal and process in boiling water bath for 20 minutes (see Preserving Basics, p. 83). Makes about 6 cups (1.5 L).

CLOSE-UP ON BEETS

Choose Well
● Small to medium-size smooth, tight-skinned firm beets with roots and fresh crisp leaves are best.

● Choose beets of uniform size for even cooking.

Quantity
● Four medium beets without leaves total about 1 lb (500 g), and yield about 2-1/2 cups (625 mL) diced, enough for 2 to 3 servings.

Storage
● Cut off leaves about 1-1/2 inches (4 cm) from beets, storing beets and leaves separately, beets for up to 2 weeks in refrigerator, leaves for 2 to 3 days. Do not cut tap roots.

Preparation
● Since beets bleed, do not cut or peel unless using in soup (see p. 59). Just gently brush off any grit, especially around stem and root end.

Cooking Basics
● Baking beets retains maximum color and flavor. To bake, wrap beets in foil or place in heatproof covered casserole dish and bake in 375°F (190°C) oven for about 1-1/2 hours or until skin can be wrinkled with blade of a knife.

● Or, cover and cook in pot of boiling water for about 30 minutes.

● When testing for doneness, avoid piercing the beets to let out juices. Do the wrinkle test to see if skins will slip off easily.

Nutrition Note
● Beets are a source of vitamin C, iron and potassium.

● Beet greens are a source of calcium, iron, potassium, vitamin C and fiber, and are very high in beta carotene.

Chili Corn Relish

4 cups	chopped ripe tomatoes	1 L
1-1/2 cups	chopped onions	375 mL
1-1/2 cups	diced sweet green pepper	375 mL
1 cup	diced celery	250 mL
1/2 cup	minced hot red or green chili peppers	125 mL
2 cups	cider vinegar	500 mL
1-1/4 cups	packed brown sugar	300 mL
4 tsp	chili powder	20 mL
1 tbsp	pickling salt	15 mL
1 tbsp	mustard seeds	15 mL
1-1/2 tsp	each ground cumin and coriander	7 mL
4 cups	corn kernels	1 L

● In large nonaluminum saucepan or Dutch oven, combine tomatoes, onions, green pepper, celery and red chili peppers. Stir in vinegar, sugar, chili powder, salt, mustard seeds, cumin and coriander; bring to boil. Reduce heat and simmer, stirring often, for 40 minutes.

● Stir in corn; cook, stirring, for 10 to 15 minutes or until corn is tender and mixture slightly thickened.

● Ladle into hot sterilized canning jars, leaving 1/2-inch (1.25 cm) headspace. Seal and process in boiling water bath for 20 minutes (see Preserving Basics, p. 83). Makes 8 cups (2 L).

This mildly hot and spicy tomato-corn relish is a bit like salsa — and, like salsa, it perks up burgers, grilled cheese and nachos.

TIP: When handling hot peppers, wear disposable rubber gloves and avoid touching any part of your body. Gloves are available in pharmacies and are worth the few pennies they cost for the number of smarting eyes, burned lips and irritated fingers they save.

Zucchini Bread and Butter Pickles

3	golden zucchini	3
4	green zucchini	4
1	small sweet red pepper, julienned	1
2	small onions, thinly sliced	2
1/4 cup	pickling salt	50 mL
24	ice cubes	24
1-1/2 cups	white vinegar	375 mL
3/4 cup	granulated sugar	175 mL
1 tbsp	mustard seeds	15 mL
1/4 tsp	each turmeric and celery seeds	1 mL

● Trim golden and green zucchini; slice thinly. In large nonaluminum bowl, combine zucchini, red pepper, onions and salt; toss well. Add ice cubes and cover with cold water; let stand for 1 to 2 hours. Drain and rinse; drain again.

● In large saucepan, combine vinegar, sugar, mustard seeds, turmeric and celery seeds; bring to boil. Add zucchini mixture and return to boil; reduce heat and simmer for about 3 minutes or until vegetables are tender-crisp.

● Ladle into hot sterilized canning jars, leaving 1/2-inch (1.25 cm) headspace. Seal and process in boiling water bath for 10 minutes (see Preserving Basics, p. 83). Makes about 4 cups (2 L).

The overabundant zucchini stands in for traditional cucumbers in this pleasing sliced pickle. The recipe suits cucumbers, too — just remember to choose slim, firm ones for even-size slices.

CLOSE-UP ON TOMATOES

Choose Well

● Choose firm unblemished tomatoes.

Quantity

● Two medium tomatoes weigh about 1 lb (500 g) and yield about 2 cups (500 mL) chopped or peeled, seeded and diced.

● One tomato yields about 7 thin slices.

Storage

● Store stems up, in single layer and without touching, at room temperature out of sunlight until brightly colored and skin yields to gentle pressure.

● Never store in the refrigerator unless tomatoes are in danger of spoiling.

Preparation

● To prepare a quantity, cut X in bottom of each tomato; place in heatproof bowl.

Cover with boiling water and let stand for about 30 seconds or until skins begin to split. Immediately drain and cool in cold water. Remove and peel, cutting out cores.

● To seed, cut in half crosswise and squeeze out seeds.

Nutrition Note

● A good source of beta carotene, vitamin C and potassium.

Keep in Mind

● Look for new colors, sizes and shapes of tomatoes — from bright yellow to pink and orange, shaped like pears, plums or globes, from tiny cherry-size to 1/2-lb (250 g) whoppers.

● Tomatoes grown locally and ripened as long as possible on the vine are tastier than imported tomatoes.

Sun-Dried Tomato Vinaigrette

2 tbsp	finely chopped sun-dried tomatoes	25 mL
2 tbsp	balsamic or red wine vinegar	25 mL
1 tsp	Dijon mustard	5 mL
1	clove garlic, minced	1
Pinch	each salt and pepper	Pinch
1/3 cup	extra virgin olive oil	75 mL

● In small bowl, whisk together tomatoes, vinegar, mustard, garlic, salt and pepper; gradually whisk in oil. Makes about 1/2 cup (125 mL).

The sunny roasted flavor of dried tomatoes goes well with leafy spring lettuce.

Tomato, Avocado and Coriander Salsa

2 cups	chopped tomatoes	500 mL
1	small red onion, chopped	1
2 tbsp	chopped fresh coriander	25 mL
2 tbsp	(approx) hot taco sauce	25 mL
1	clove garlic, chopped	1
1/2 tsp	chopped fresh thyme	2 mL
2	avocados	2
	Salt	

● In bowl, combine tomatoes, onion, coriander, taco sauce, garlic and thyme. *(Salsa can be prepared to this point and refrigerated for up to 3 hours.)*

● Peel, pit and chop avocados into small pieces; toss with tomato mixture. Season with more taco sauce and salt to taste. Makes about 4 cups (1 L).

Plan this salsa for tacos, or serve over grilled, steamed or pan-fried fish.

Quick 'n' Easy Pickle Slices

3 cups	thinly sliced English cucumbers	750 mL
1/2 cup	thinly sliced red onion	125 mL
1/4 cup	granulated sugar	50 mL
1/4 cup	white vinegar	50 mL
Half	sweet green pepper, slivered	Half
1 tsp	pickling salt	5 mL
3/4 tsp	celery seeds	4 mL

● In large bowl, mix together cucumbers, onion, sugar, vinegar, green pepper, salt and celery seeds; let stand for 30 minutes, tossing occasionally. *(Pickles can be covered and refrigerated for up to 1 day.)* Makes about 3 cups (750 mL).

You might call these overnight pickles since the cucumber marinates for only 1 day before reaching pickling perfection. Try these slices for a burger party.

Fresh Cucumber Relish

This instant relish is a cooling condiment for spicy Indian food as well as an accompaniment for salmon, trout or any other fish that's firm enough to grill. Keep it in mind for burgers, too.

1-1/2 cups	finely diced English cucumber	375 mL
1/2 cup	finely diced Spanish onion	125 mL
1 tbsp	finely chopped fresh mint	15 mL
1 tbsp	white wine vinegar	15 mL
1 tsp	granulated sugar	5 mL
1/2 tsp	grated lemon rind	2 mL
	Salt and pepper	

● In small bowl, combine cucumber, onion, mint, vinegar, sugar, lemon rind, and salt and pepper to taste. *(Relish can be covered and refrigerated for up to 8 hours.)* Makes 1-1/2 cups (375 mL).

Cucumber Dill Sauce

Dress up grilled or broiled fish with this quick, fresh-tasting sauce.

1/3 cup	shredded peeled English cucumber	75 mL
1/4 cup	mayonnaise	50 mL
1/4 cup	plain yogurt	50 mL
1	green onion, sliced	1
2 tsp	chopped fresh dill	10 mL

● In small bowl, combine cucumber, mayonnaise, yogurt, onion and dill. *(Sauce can be covered and refrigerated for up to 2 days.)* Makes 3/4 cup (175 mL).

CLOSE-UP ON PEPPERS

Choose Well
● Look for peppers with a glossy, firm, unblemished skin.

Quantity
● A sweet bell pepper weighs about 6 oz

(175 g) and produces about 1 cup (250 mL) chopped.

● Hot peppers weigh mere ounces or grams and the amount used depends on personal taste.

Storage
● Store in plastic bag in crisper for up to 5 days.

● Red peppers are riper than green and do not keep as well.

Preparation
● Rinse, cut out core and remove membranes and seeds.

● When handling hot peppers, remember to wear rubber gloves to protect hands and other body parts from burns.

Cooking Basics
● Grilling, sautéeing, stir-frying and roasting suit sweet peppers best.

Nutrition Note
● All peppers are rich in vitamin C. Red peppers also contribute beta carotene.

Keep in Mind
● The smaller the pepper, the hotter it is.

● Sweet bell peppers ripen from green to red, sweetening as they mature, with some varieties ripening to yellow, orange, brown and even purple.

Roasted Red Pepper Mayo

2	sweet red peppers	2
1/2 cup	light mayonnaise	125 mL
2 tsp	red wine vinegar	10 mL
Pinch	cayenne pepper	Pinch

● Broil or grill red peppers, turning several times, for about 20 minutes or until blistered and charred all over. Let cool; peel and seed.

● In food processor, purée peppers. Add mayonnaise, vinegar and cayenne; process until combined. *(Mayonnaise can be refrigerated for up to 1 day in airtight container.)* Makes 1-1/2 cups (375 mL).

TIP: When there's no time to roast peppers, you can substitute 1 cup (250 mL) diced bottled roasted peppers, drained.

This creamy orange-colored mayonnaise is heaven with chicken burgers, grilled salmon and lamb.

Roasted Red Peppers with Oregano

4	sweet red peppers	4
1/4 cup	lemon juice	50 mL
1	large clove garlic, chopped	1
1/2 cup	extra virgin olive oil	125 mL
2 tbsp	chopped fresh oregano	25 mL
	Salt and pepper	

● Broil or grill red peppers, turning several times, for about 20 minutes or until blistered and charred all over. Let cool; peel, seed and cut into strips.

● In bowl, combine lemon juice with garlic; gradually whisk in oil. Add oregano, and salt and pepper to taste. Stir in red pepper; toss to coat.

● Cover and let stand at room temperature for 1 hour before serving. *(Peppers can be refrigerated in airtight container for up to 1 week.)* Makes about 2 cups (500 mL).

This is more like a roasted red pepper salad than a preserve or sauce, and is absolutely wonderful served over open-faced goat cheese sandwiches. Or, toss a few of the pepper strips onto a pizza or bruschetta.

Tahini Dressing and Dip

1/2 cup	tahini	125 mL
1/3 cup	lemon juice	75 mL
1/4 cup	extra virgin olive oil	50 mL
1/4 cup	water	50 mL
1	clove garlic, minced	1
1/2 tsp	ground cumin	2 mL
1/4 tsp	hot pepper sauce	1 mL
1/4 tsp	salt	1 mL

● In small bowl, stir together tahini, lemon juice, oil and water until smooth; stir in garlic, cumin, hot pepper sauce and salt. Makes about 1 cup (250 mL).

Tahini is ground sesame seeds made into a sauce. Enjoy its nutty flavor with roasted vegetables or grilled or steamed fish — or use it as a tasty dip with crudités (see p. 65).

The Contributors

For your easy reference, we have included an alphabetical listing of recipes by contributor.

Elizabeth Baird
Balsamic Roasted Onions, 24
Eggplant Rolls with Quick Tomato Sauce, 22
Fairouz Salad, 79
Fresh and Spicy Squash Soup, 50
Grilled Peppers with Shaved Asiago, 64
Honey-Orange Beets, 32
Italian Potato Croquettes, 64
Leek and Potato Soup, 56
Mellow Onion and Provolone Pizza, 12
Microwave Spaghetti Squash with Cheese, 9
Mustard Mayo-Glazed Tomato Slices, 49
Parsnip and Cheddar Soup, 55
Roasted Tomatoes, 66
Ruby Beet Chutney, 84
Sesame Spinach with Mushrooms, 42
Skinny Buttermilk Mashed Potatoes, 48
Sliced Potato Pizza, 12
Spicy Pearl Onion Sours, 80
Spinach Sensation, 75
Stir-Fried Sweet and Sour Carrots, 29
Sweet and Sour Pearls, 24
Sweet Peppers with Rice and Sausage, 6
Taco Sauce, 82
Tomato and Basil Tart, 19
Tomato Red Pepper Pasta, 9
Zucchini Bread and Butter Pickles, 85

Johanna Burkhard
Chili Corn Relish, 85

Janet Cornish
Cornmeal Corn Pancakes, 10

Cynthia David
Cucumber Dill Sauce, 88
Fresh Cucumber Relish, 88

Nancy Enright
Cauliflower and Broccoli Medley, 11
Roasted Red Pepper Mayo, 89
Roasted Red Peppers with Oregano, 89
Tomato, Avocado and Coriander Salsa, 87
Warmed Tomatoes with Basil and Brie, 49

Shannon Ferrier and Tamara Shuttleworth
Prizewinning Chili Sauce, 83

Margaret Fraser
Asparagus Frittata, 16
Light Vegetable Pasta Salad, 76

Anne Lindsay
Bodybuilder Broccoli Salad, 75
Grilled Vegetable Salad, 73
Light and Creamy Broccoli Soup, 60
Salade Composée, 74
Sesame Carrots, 26
Spinach with Lemon and Nutmeg, 41
Zucchini, Potato and Egg Skillet Supper, 16

Rose Murray
Carrot Pilaf, 29
Cheddar Carrot Soup, 58
Cheddar-Corn Impossible Pie, 19
Cream of Fiddlehead Soup, 58
Creamed Carrots and Onions, 27
15-Minute Tomato Soup, 53
Garlicky Broccoli Pasta, 9
Golden Rutabaga Casserole, 34
Green Tomato Hotdog Relish, 82
Mustardy Brussels Sprouts, 38
Skillet Asparagus with Mushrooms, 43
Skinny Buttermilk Mashed Potatoes, 48
Spinach Sensation, 75
Stir-Fried Green Beans and Sweet Peppers, 45
Sweet Peppers with Rice and Sausage, 6
The Very Best Home Fries, 48
Tomato Salad Provençale, 76

Daphna Rabinovitch
Potato Casserole with Cheese and Mushrooms, 15
Tomato Bread Soup, 54

Michelle Ramsay
Orange Sesame Asparagus and Greens, 72

Iris Raven
Buttercup Squash and Apple Casserole, 33
Cabbage Roll Casserole, 10
Carrots Moroccan-Style, 30
Gingery Orange Squash Toss, 33
Vegetarian Cabbage Rolls, 10

Terry Seed
Fried Red Tomatoes, 49
Plum Tomato and Capocollo
Flan, 17

Bertha Skye
Three Sisters Soup, 52

Kay Spicer
Green Bean Salad with
Julienne of Turkey, 78

Bonnie Stern
Caramelized Beets and
Onions, 32
Curry Glazed Carrots, 29
Grilled Pepper and Fennel
Salad, 79
Herbed Potato Casserole, 48
Parsnip-Carrot Purée with
Apricots, 31
Roasted Root Vegetables, 31
Tomato Salsa with Peppered
Cheese, 65

Anita Stewart
Curried Winter
Vegetables, 23

Lucy Waverman
Asparagus with Creamy
Orange Vinaigrette, 43

Herbed Onions and
Mushrooms, 26
Red Cabbage with
Cranberries, 38

**Canadian Living
Test Kitchen**
A Trio of Summer Dips, 62
Beet and Pear Purée, 32
Bowl-of-Jewels Borscht, 59
Broccoli Slaw, 70
Celery Root Soup, 55
Corn Custard Pudding, 10
Corn Soup with Red Pepper
Swirl, 53
Creamed Carrot Soup, 57
Creamy Gaucamole, 65
Curried Corn and Chicken
Salad, 76
Curried Zucchini Soup, 59
Easy Garden Risotto, 8
Fennel Gratin, 42
Fiesta Cheesecake, 69
Garden Vegetable Platter, 36
Green Beans Gremolata, 45
Green Beans with Asian
Flair, 45
Honey-Glazed Rutabaga, 34

Leek Tart, 21
Light and Creamy
Spinach, 41
Maple Brussels Sprouts
with Onions, 40
Pesto Cucumber
Gazpacho, 56
Potato and Mushroom
Strudel, 14
Potato Salad Roll, 72
Potatoes Anna, 47
Puréed Parsnips with
Cumin, 31
Quick 'n' Easy Pickle
Slices, 87
Red Barn Corn and Bean
Salad, 77
Roasted Vegetable Stock, 61
Sicilian Broccoli, 39
Spinach and Cheese Phyllo
Triangles, 66
Steamed Cauliflower with
Thyme Vinaigrette, 40
Stir-Fried Cabbage, 39
Summertime Potato
Salad, 70
Sun-Dried Tomato
Vinaigrette, 87
Tahini Dressing and Dip, 89
Turkish Eggplant, 35
Two-Toned Grilled Onion
Slices, 16

Photography Credits

LAURA ARSIE:
photo of Elizabeth Baird.

FRED BIRD:
back cover (top inset), pages
7, 11, 13, 17, 18, 23, 25, 28,
30, 41, 44, 52, 60, 63, 67, 68,
71, 73, 74, 78, 81, 86, 88.

CHRISTOPHER
CAMPBELL: page 77.

CHRISTOPHER DEW:
photo of Test Kitchen staff.

DAVE FIELD: page 33.

FRESH FOR FLAVOUR
FOUNDATION, OTTAWA:
page 84.

MIKE VISSER: page 57.

MICHAEL WARING:
pages 15, 46, 54.

ROBERT WIGINGTON:
front cover, back cover
(bottom insets), pages
4, 8, 21, 37, 43, 51.

Special Thanks

Canadian Living's Best series grows with the Spring 1995 titles, enriched with new contributors, and steadied by the experienced hand of project editor Wanda Nowakowska, Canadian Living's senior editor, Beverley Renahan, and Test Kitchen director Daphna Rabinovitch. All have contributed their expertise and attention to detail to every page. In the Test Kitchen, Dana McCauley created many of the new recipes, assisted by staff members Heather Howe, Jennifer MacKenzie, Kate Gammel and former staffers Jan Main and Donna Bartolini. Senior editor Donna Paris shaped many of the recipes when they first appeared in Canadian Living magazine.

We prize the delicious recipes created first by writers, especially our longtime contributors — Marg Fraser, Carol Ferguson, Rose Murray, Iris Raven, Kay Spicer and Bonnie Stern — joined by writer and our nutrition editor, Anne Lindsay. We are thankful for the help of Olga Goncalves, Rosemary Hillary and Tina Gaudino who facilitate the works in progress. Thanks go also to Canadian Living's art director, Martha Weaver, and former art director Deborah Fadden who have overseen almost all of the photography in this series. Our thanks to photographers Michael Waring, Robert Wigington, Michael Visser, Christopher Campbell and Fred Bird for their luscious shots. Some new names have joined our food stylists, Olga Truchan and Jennifer McLagan; they include Claire Stancer, Ruth Gangbar, Debbie Charendoff Moses, Rosemarie Superville, Kathy Robertson and Sharon Dale. And when everyone else has finished arranging the recipes, the food, angles, props and lighting, book designer Gord Sibley puts the pages together so they're a treat to look at, but more important, easy to read and cook from. A heartfelt thanks and bravo to you all, and to Canadian Living editor-in-chief Bonnie Cowan and associate publisher Caren King. Their support of the Best series is valued.

Elizabeth Baird

Index

*O*ver 100 recipes bursting
with gardenfresh flavor.

**STOCK
EXCHANGE**
Throughout this book,
vegetable stock can be
substituted for chicken
or beef stock.

A

APPETIZERS
  Cheesecake, Fiesta, 69
  Eggplant Dip, Grilled, 62
  Guacamole, Creamy, 65
  Hummus, Creamy, 62
  Onions, Balsamic
    Roasted, 24
  Onions, Sweet and Sour
    Pearls, 24
  Onions, Two-Tone
    Grilled Slices, 26
  Peppers, Grilled, with
    Shaved Asiago, 64
  Potato Croquettes,
    Italian, 64
  Spinach and Cheese
    Phyllo Triangles, 66
  Tomato Salsa with
    Peppered Cheese, 65
  Tomatoes, Roasted, 66
  Tzatziki, Minted, 62

Asparagus
  basics, 43
  Easy Garden Risotto, 8
  Frittata, 16
  Garden Vegetable
    Platter, 36
  Orange Sesame, and
    Greens, 72
  Skillet, with
    Mushrooms, 43
  with Creamy Orange
    Vinaigrette, 43
Avocados
  Tomato, Avocado and
    Coriander Salsa, 87
  Creamy Guacamole, 65

B

Beans
  basics, 44
  Garden Vegetable
    Platter, 36
  Green Bean Salad with
    Julienne of Turkey, 78
  Green Beans
    Gremolata, 45
  Green Beans with Asian
    Flair, 45
  Stir-Fried Green Beans
    and Sweet Peppers, 45
  Three Sisters Soup, 52
Beef
  Cabbage Roll
    Casserole, 10
Beets
  basics, 84
  Beet and Pear Purée, 32
  Bowl-of-Jewels
    Borscht, 59
  Caramelized Beets and
    Onions, 32
  Honey-Orange, 32
  Ruby Chutney, 84
  Salade Composée, 74
Broccoli
  basics, 39
  Bodybuilder Salad, 75
  Cauliflower and Broccoli
    Medley, 11
  Garlicky Broccoli Pasta, 9
  Light and Creamy
    Soup, 60
  Light Vegetable Pasta
    Salad, 76
  Sicilian, 39
  Slaw, 70
Brussels Sprouts
  basics, 40
  Maple, with Onions, 40
  Mustardy, 38

C

Cabbage
  basics, 38
  Cabbage Roll
    Casserole, 10
  Curried Corn and
    Chicken Salad, 76
  Red, with Cranberries, 38
  Stir-Fried, 39
  Vegetarian Cabbage
    Rolls, 10

CARROTS
  basics, 27
  Main Dishes
  Cabbage Roll
    Casserole, 10
  Curried Winter
    Vegetables, 23
  Easy Garden Risotto, 8
  Vegetarian Cabbage
    Rolls, 10
  Salads
  Broccoli Slaw, 70
  Curried Corn and
    Chicken Salad, 76
  Light Vegetable Pasta
    Salad, 76
  Salade Composée, 74
  Soups
  Bowl-of-Jewels
    Borscht, 59
  Cheddar Carrot, 58
  Creamed, with
    Coriander, 57
  Roasted Vegetable
    Stock, 61
  Side Dishes
  Creamed Carrots and
    Onions, 27
  Curry Glazed, 29
  Golden Rutabaga
    Casserole, 34
  Moroccan-Style, 30
  Parsnip-Carrot Purée
    with Apricots, 31
  Pilaf, 29

Roasted Root Vegetables, 31
Sesame, 26
Stir-Fried Sweet And Sour, 29

CASSEROLES
Buttercup Squash and Apple, 33
Cabbage Roll, 10
Cabbage Rolls, Vegetarian, 10
Carrots and Onions, Creamed, 27
Cauliflower and Broccoli Medley, 11
Eggplant Rolls, 22
Eggplant, Turkish, 35
Fennel Gratin, 42
Potato with Cheese and Mushrooms, 15
Potato, Herbed, 48
Potatoes Anna, 47
Rutabaga, Golden, 34

Cauliflower
basics, 11
Cauliflower and Broccoli Medley, 11
Curried Winter Vegetables, 23
Steamed with Thyme Vinaigrette, 40

Celery
Bowl-of-Jewels Borscht, 59
Roasted Vegetable Stock, 61
Root Soup with Parsnip Chips, 55

CHEESE
Asparagus Frittata, 16
Carrot and Cheddar Soup, 58
Cauliflower and Broccoli Medley, 11
Cheesecake, Fiesta, 69
Corn Custard Pudding, 20
Corn-Cheddar Impossible Pie, 19
Eggplant Rolls, 22
Onion and Provolone Pizza, 12
Parsnip and Cheddar Soup, 55
Peppers, Grilled, with Shaved Asiago, 64

Potato Casserole with Cheese and Mushrooms, 15
Potato Casserole, Herbed, 48
Potato Croquettes, Italian, 64
Spaghetti Squash, Microwave, 9
Spinach and Cheese Phyllo Triangles, 66
Tomato and Basil Tart, 19
Tomato and Capocollo Flan, 17
Tomato Salsa with Peppered Cheese, 65
Tomatoes, Warmed, with Basil and Brie, 49

Chicken
Curried Corn and Chicken Salad, 76

Chutney
Ruby Beet, 84

Corn
basics, 52
15-Minute Tomato Soup, 53
Cheddar-Corn Impossible Pie, 19
Chili Corn Relish, 85
Cornmeal Pancakes, 20
Curried Corn and Chicken Salad, 76
Custard Pudding, 20
Red Barn Corn and Bean Salad, 77
Salade Composée, 74
Soup with Red Pepper Swirl, 53
Three Sisters Soup, 52

Cucumbers
Dill Sauce, 88
Fairouz Salad, 79
Fresh Relish, 88
Green Tomato Hotdog Relish, 82
Minted Tzatziki, 62
Pesto Gazpacho, 56
Quick 'n' Easy Pickle Slices, 87

D

Dips
Creamy Hummus, 62
Creamy Guacamole, 65
Grilled Eggplant, 62
Minted Tzatziki, 62
Tahini, 89

Dressings
Roasted Red Pepper Mayo, 89
Sun-Dried Tomato Vinaigrette, 87
Tahini, 89

E

Eggplant
basics, 35
Garden Vegetable Platter, 36
Grilled Dip, 62
Grilled Vegetable Salad, 72
Rolls with Quick Tomato Sauce, 22
Turkish, 35

EGGS
Asparagus Frittata, 16
Corn Custard Pudding, 20
Corn-Cheddar Impossible Pie, 19
Leek Tart, 21
Potato Salad Roll, 72
Spinach Sensation, 75
Tomato and Basil Tart, 19
Tomatoes, Fried Red, 49
Zucchini, Potato and Egg Skillet Supper, 16

F

Fennel
Gratin, 42
Grilled Pepper and Fennel Salad, 79

Fiddleheads
Cream Soup, 58

Frittata
Asparagus, 16

G

Green Beans. *See* **Beans.**

Guacamole
Creamy, 65

H

Ham
Cauliflower and Broccoli Medley, 11
Plum Tomato and Capocollo Flan, 17

Hummus
Creamy, 62

I

INFORMATION
Asparagus, 43
Beans, 44
Beets, 84
Broccoli, 39
Brussels Sprouts, 40
Cabbage, 38
Carrots, 27
Cauliflower, 11
Corn, 52
Eggplant, 35
Herb Garnishes, 50
Leeks, 20
New Veggies for Dipping, 65
Onions, 80
Peas, 33
Potatoes, 14
Preserving, 83
Rutabaga, 34
Soup Toppers, 61
Spinach, 42
Summer Squash, 36
Sweet Potatoes, 47
Tomatoes, 86
Turnips, 34
Vegetable Quick Tricks, 16
Vegetable Stock, 56
Winter Squash, 23

L

Leeks
basics, 20
Celery Root Soup, 55
Cream of Fiddlehead Soup, 58

Tart, 21
Tomato Bread Soup, 54
Vegetarian Cabbage
   Rolls, 10

M

Mayonnaise
   Roasted Red Pepper, 89
Microwave
   Spaghetti Squash with
      Cheese, 9
Mushrooms
   Herbed Onions and
      Mushrooms, 26
   Potato Casserole, 15
   Potato Strudel, 14
   Sesame Spinach, 42
   Skillet Asparagus, 43

O

ONIONS
   basics, 80
   Appetizers
   Fiesta Cheesecake, 69
   Tomato Salsa with
      Peppered Cheese, 65
   Tomato, Avocado and
      Coriander Salsa, 87
   Main Dishes
   Cabbage Roll
      Casserole, 10
   Easy Garden Risotto, 8
   Mellow Onion and
      Provolone Pizza, 12
   Sweet Peppers with Rice
      and Sausage, 6
   Preserves
   Chili Corn Relish, 85
   Green Tomato Hotdog
      Relish, 82
   Prizewinning Chili
      Sauce, 83
   Ruby Beet Chutney, 84
   Taco Sauce, 82
   Zucchini Bread and
      Butter Pickles, 85
   Soups
   15-Minute Tomato, 53
   Bowl-of-Jewels
      Borscht, 59
   Corn, with Red Pepper
      Swirl, 53
   Cream of Fiddlehead, 58
   Curried Zucchini, 59

Fresh and Spicy
   Squash, 50
Parsnip and Cheddar, 55
Roasted Vegetable
   Stock, 61
Salads
   Fairouz, 79
   Summertime Potato, 70
Side Dishes
   Balsamic Roasted, 24
   Beet and Pear Purée, 32
   Caramelized Beets and
      Onions, 32
   Creamed Carrots and
      Onions, 27
   Herbed Onions and
      Mushrooms, 26
   Maple Brussels
      Sprouts, 40
   Red Cabbage with
      Cranberries, 38
   Roasted Root
      Vegetables, 31
   Spicy Pearl Sours, 80
   Stir-Fried Cabbage, 39
   Stir-Fried Sweet And
      Sour Carrots, 29
   Sweet and Sour
      Pearls, 24
   Turkish Eggplant, 35
   Two-Tone Grilled
      Slices, 26

P

Pancakes
   Cornmeal Corn, 20
Parsnips
   Celery Root Soup, 55
   Parsnip and Cheddar
      Soup, 55
   Parsnip-Carrot Purée
      with Apricots, 31
   Puréed, with Cumin, 31
   Roasted Root
      Vegetables, 31
Pasta
   Garlicky Broccoli, 9
   Light Vegetable Salad, 76
   Tomato Red Pepper, 9
Peas
   basics, 33
   Easy Garden Risotto, 8

PEPPERS
   Appetizers
   Fiesta Cheesecake, 69
   Grilled, with Shaved
      Asiago, 64

Main Dishes
   Sliced Potato Pizza, 12
   Tomato Red Pepper
      Pasta, 9
   with Rice and Sausage, 6
Preserves and Sauces
   Chili Corn Relish, 85
   Green Tomato Hotdog
      Relish, 82
   Prizewinning Chili
      Sauce, 83
   Roasted Red Pepper
      Mayo, 89
   Zucchini Bread and
      Butter Pickles, 85
Salads
   Curried Corn and
      Chicken, 76
   Fairouz, 79
   Garden Vegetable
      Platter, 36
   Grilled Pepper and
      Fennel, 79
   Grilled Vegetable, 72
   Red Barn Corn and
      Bean, 77
   Roasted Red, with
      Oregano, 89
Soups
   Corn, with Red Pepper
      Swirl, 53
Side Dishes
   Stir-Fried Cabbage, 39
   Stir-Fried Green Beans
      and Sweet Peppers, 45

Pesto
   Cucumber Gazpacho, 56
Pickles
   Quick 'n' Easy Slices, 87
   Zucchini Bread and
      Butter, 85
Pizza
   Mellow Onion and
      Provolone, 12
   Sliced Potato, 12

POTATOES
   basics, 14
   Appetizers
   Italian Croquettes, 64
   Hand Warmers, 64
   Main Dishes
   Cabbage Roll
      Casserole, 10
   Casserole with Cheese
      and Mushrooms, 15
   Curried Winter
      Vegetables. 23

Mushroom Strudel, 14
Sliced Potato Pizza, 12
Zucchini and Egg Skillet
   Supper, 16
Soups
   Bowl-of-Jewels
      Borscht, 59
   Leek and Potato, 56
   Light and Creamy
      Broccoli, 60
   Three Sisters, 52
Salads
   Potato Salad Roll, 72
   Salade Composée, 74
   Summertime Potato, 70
Side Dishes
   Potatoes Anna, 47
   Herbed Casserole, 48
   Parsnip-Carrot Purée
      with Apricots, 31
   Skinny Buttermilk
      Mashed, 48
   Very Best Home Fries, 48

Preserves
   basics, 83
   Chili Corn Relish, 85
   Green Tomato Hotdog
      Relish, 82
   Prizewinning Chili
      Sauce, 83
   Ruby Beet Chutney, 84
   Spicy Pearl Onion
      Sours, 80
   Taco Sauce, 82
   Zucchini Bread and
      Butter Pickles, 85

Q

Quiches and Tarts
   Cheddar-Corn Impossible
      Pie, 19
   Leek Tart, 21
   Tomato and Basil
      Tart, 19

R

Radishes
   Broccoli Slaw, 70
   Fairouz Salad, 79
   Summertime Potato
      Salad, 70
Relish
   Chili Corn, 85
   Fresh Cucumber, 88

Green Tomato Hotdog, 82
Rice
Carrot Pilaf, 29
Easy Garden Risotto, 8
Sweet Peppers with Rice
and Sausage, 6
Vegetarian Cabbage
Rolls, 10
Risotto
Easy Garden, 8
Rutabaga
basics, 34
Golden Casserole, 34
Honey-Glazed, 34
Roasted Root
Vegetables, 31
Vegetarian Cabbage
Rolls, 10

S

SALADS
Asparagus and
Greens, 72
Broccoli Slaw, 70
Broccoli, Bodybuilder, 75
Composée, 74
Corn and Bean, Red
Barn, 77
Corn and Chicken,
Curried, 76
Fairouz, 79
Green Bean, with
Julienne of Turkey, 78
Pepper, Grilled, and
Fennel, 79
Potato Salad Roll, 72
Potato, Summertime, 70
Spinach Sensation, 75
Tomato Provençale, 76
Vegetable Pasta, Light, 76
Vegetable, Grilled 73

Salsa
Fiesta Cheesecake, 69
Tomato, with Peppered
Cheese, 65
Tomato, Avocado and
Coriander, 87
Sauces
Cucumber Dill, 88
Prizewinning Chili, 83
Taco, 82
Sausages
Cabbage Roll
Casserole, 10
Sweet Peppers with Rice
and Sausage, 6

SOUPS
Bowl-of-Jewels
Borscht, 59
Celery Root, with Parsnip
Chips, 55
Carrot Cheddar, 58
Cream of Fiddlehead, 58
Creamed Carrot with
Coriander, 57
Curried Zucchini, 59
Fresh and Spicy
Squash, 50
Leek and Potato, 56
Light and Creamy
Broccoli, 60
Roasted Vegetable
Stock, 61
Tomato Bread, 54

Spinach
basics, 42
Light and Creamy, 41
Sensation, 75
Sesame, with
Mushrooms, 42
Spinach and Cheese
Phyllo Triangles, 66
with Lemon and
Nutmeg, 41

SQUASH
Summer
basics, 36
15-Minute Tomato
Soup, 53
Curried Zucchini
Soup, 59
Garden Vegetable
Platter, 36
Grilled Vegetable
Salad, 73
Zucchini Bread and
Butter Pickles, 85
Zucchini, Potato and Egg
Skillet Supper, 16
Winter
basics, 23
Buttercup Squash and
Apple Casserole, 33
Curried Winter
Vegetables, 23
Fresh and Spicy Soup, 50
Gingery Orange Toss, 33
Microwave Spaghetti
Squash with Cheese, 9
Three Sisters Soup, 52

Stock
Roasted Vegetable, 61
Sweet Potatoes
basics, 47
Potatoes Anna, 47

T

Tahini
Dressing and Dip, 89
Tarts. *See* **Quiches and
Tarts.**

TOMATOES
basics, 86
sun-dried, 17
Appetizers
Fiesta Cheesecake, 69
Roasted, 66
Salsa with Peppered
Cheese, 65
Tomato, Avocado and
Coriander Salsa, 87
Main Dishes
Eggplant Rolls with
Quick Tomato
Sauce, 22
Plum Tomato and
Capocollo Flan, 17
Red Pepper Pasta, 9
Sweet Peppers with Rice
and Sausage, 6
Tomato and Basil
Tart, 19
Preserves
Chili Corn Relish, 85
Green Tomato Hotdog
Relish, 82
Prizewinning Chili
Sauce, 83
Taco Sauce, 82
Soups
15-Minute, 53
Bowl-of-Jewels
Borscht, 59
Fresh and Spicy
Squash, 50
Pesto Cucumber
Gazpacho, 56
Roasted Vegetable
Stock, 61
Tomato Bread, 54
Salads
Fairouz, 79
Green Bean, with
Julienne of Turkey, 78
Provençale, 76
Sun-Dried Vinaigrette, 87

Side Dishes
Fried Red, 49
Garden Vegetable
Platter, 36
Mustard Mayo-Glazed
Slices, 49
Turkish Eggplant, 35
Warmed, with Basil and
Brie, 49

Turnips
basics, 34
Honey-Glazed, 34
Tzatziki
Minted, 62

V

Vinaigrette
Sun-Dried Tomato, 87

Z

Zucchini
Bread and Butter
Pickles, 85
Curried Soup, 59
15-Minute Tomato Soup,
53
Garden Vegetable
Platter, 36
Grilled Vegetable
Salad, 72
Potato and Egg Skillet
Supper, 16

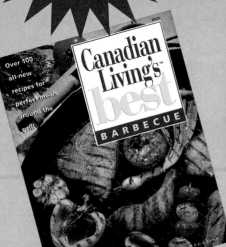
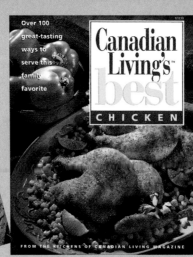
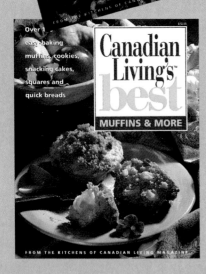